ANNA MACKMIN

Anna Mackmin's first novel *Devoured* was published by Propolis. It was shortlisted for the Desmond Elliott Prize, won the New Angle Book of the Year and the East Anglian award for Best Novel.

Directing work includes: *The Divine Mrs S* (Hampstead Theatre); *Woman in Mind* (Chichester Festival Theatre); *Di and Viv and Rose* (Hampstead Theatre/Vaudeville Theatre); *Hedda Gabler*, *The Real Thing*, *Dancing at Lughnasa* (Old Vic); *Intolerance* (from *Shoot / Get Treasure / Repeat*), *Really Old Like Forty-Five*, *Chatroom*, *Burn*, *Citizenship* (National Theatre); *Ghosts* (Gate Theatre, London); *Hedda Gabler* (Gate Theatre, Dublin); *In Celebration*, *Under the Blue Sky* (Duke of York's Theatre); *Dying for It*, *The Lightning Play* (Almeida); *The Dark* (Donmar Warehouse); *Mammals* (Bush Theatre/tour); *Breathing Corpses*, *Food Chain* (Royal Court); *Auntie and Me* (Assembly Rooms, Edinburgh/Gaiety Theatre, Dublin); *In Flame* (Bush Theatre/New Ambassadors Theatre); *Airswimming* (Battersea Arts Centre/tour); *Me and My Girl*, *The Crucible*, *Cloud Nine*, *Iphigenia*, *Teeth 'n' Smiles* and *The Arbor* (Sheffield Crucible Theatre).

Other Titles in this Series

Waleed Akhtar
THE ART OF ILLUSION *after* Alexis Michalik
KABUL GOES POP: MUSIC TELEVISION AFGHANISTAN
THE P WORD
THE REAL ONES

Chris Bush
THE ASSASSINATION OF KATIE HOPKINS *with* Matt Winkworth
THE CHANGING ROOM
CHRIS BUSH PLAYS: ONE
A DOLL'S HOUSE *after* Ibsen
FAUSTUS: THAT DAMNED WOMAN
HUNGRY
JANE EYRE *after* Brontë
THE LAST NOËL
OTHERLAND
ROBIN HOOD AND THE CHRISTMAS HEIST
ROCK / PAPER / SCISSORS
STANDING AT THE SKY'S EDGE *with* Richard Hawley
STEEL

Jez Butterworth
THE FERRYMAN
THE HILLS OF CALIFORNIA
JERUSALEM
JEZ BUTTERWORTH PLAYS: ONE
JEZ BUTTERWORTH PLAYS: TWO
MOJO
THE NIGHT HERON
PARLOUR SONG
THE RIVER
THE WINTERLING

Caryl Churchill
BLUE HEART
CHURCHILL PLAYS: THREE
CHURCHILL PLAYS: FOUR
CHURCHILL PLAYS: FIVE
CHURCHILL: SHORTS
CLOUD NINE
DING DONG THE WICKED
A DREAM PLAY *after* Strindberg
DRUNK ENOUGH TO SAY I LOVE YOU?
ESCAPED ALONE
FAR AWAY
GLASS. KILL. BLUEBEARD'S FRIENDS. IMP.
HERE WE GO
HOTEL
ICECREAM
LIGHT SHINING IN BUCKINGHAMSHIRE
LOVE AND INFORMATION
MAD FOREST
A NUMBER
PIGS AND DOGS
SEVEN JEWISH CHILDREN
THE SKRIKER
THIS IS A CHAIR
THYESTES *after* Seneca
TRAPS
WHAT IF IF ONLY

Virginia Gay
CYRANO *after* Rostand

Branden Jacobs-Jenkins
APPROPRIATE
THE COMEUPPANCE
GLORIA
AN OCTOROON

Lucy Kirkwood
BEAUTY AND THE BEAST *with* Katie Mitchell
BLOODY WIMMIN
THE CHILDREN
CHIMERICA
HEDDA *after* Ibsen
THE HUMAN BODY
IT FELT EMPTY WHEN THE HEART WENT AT FIRST BUT IT IS ALRIGHT NOW
LUCY KIRKWOOD PLAYS: ONE
MOSQUITOES
NSFW
RAPTURE
TINDERBOX
THE WELKIN

Benedict Lombe
LAVA
SHIFTERS

Winsome Pinnock
LEAVE TAKING
PIG HEART BOY *after* Malorie Blackman
ROCKETS AND BLUE LIGHTS
TAKEN
TITUBA

Jack Thorne
2ND MAY 1997
AFTER LIFE
BUNNY
BURYING YOUR BROTHER IN THE PAVEMENT
A CHRISTMAS CAROL *after* Dickens
THE END OF HISTORY…
HOPE
JACK THORNE PLAYS: ONE
JACK THORNE PLAYS: TWO
JUNKYARD
LET THE RIGHT ONE IN *after* John Ajvide Lindqvist
THE MOTIVE AND THE CUE
MYDIDAE
THE SOLID LIFE OF SUGAR WATER
STACY & FANNY AND FAGGOT
WHEN WINSTON WENT TO WAR WITH THE WIRELESS
WHEN YOU CURE ME
WOYZECK *after* Büchner

debbie tucker green
BORN BAD
DEBBIE TUCKER GREEN PLAYS: ONE
DIRTY BUTTERFLY
EAR FOR EYE
HANG
NUT
A PROFOUNDLY AFFECTIONATE, PASSIONATE DEVOTION TO SOMEONE (– *NOUN*)
RANDOM
STONING MARY
TRADE & GENERATIONS
TRUTH AND RECONCILIATION

Phoebe Waller-Bridge
FLEABAG

Ross Willis
WOLFIE
WONDER BOY

Anna Mackmin

BACKSTROKE

NICK HERN BOOKS
London
www.nickhernbooks.co.uk

▲ Nick Hern Book

Backstroke first published in Great Britain in 2025 as a paperback original by Nick Hern Books Limited, The Glasshouse, 49a Goldhawk Road, London W12 8QP

Backstroke copyright © 2025 Anna Mackmin

Anna Mackmin has asserted her right to be identified as the author of this work

Front cover: AKA

Designed and typeset by Nick Hern Books, London
Printed in Great Britain by Mimeo Ltd, Huntingdon, Cambridgeshire PE29 6XX

A CIP catalogue record for this book is available from the British Library

ISBN 978 1 83904 399 4

CAUTION All rights whatsoever in this play are strictly reserved. Requests to reproduce the text in whole or in part should be addressed to the publisher.

Amateur Performing Rights Applications for performance, including readings and excerpts, by amateurs in the English language throughout the world should be addressed to the Performing Rights Manager, Nick Hern Books, The Glasshouse, 49a Goldhawk Road, London W12 8QP, *tel* +44 (0)20 8749 4953, *email* rights@nickhernbooks.co.uk, except as follows:

Australia: ORiGiN Theatrical, *email* enquiries@originmusic.com.au, *web* www.origintheatrical.com.au

New Zealand: Play Bureau, 20 Rua Street, Mangapapa, Gisborne, 4010, *tel* +64 21 258 3998, *email* info@playbureau.com

United States of America and Canada: Curtis Brown Ltd, see details below.

Professional Performing Rights Application for performance by professionals in any medium and in any language throughout the world should be addressed to Curtis Brown Ltd, Cunard House, 15 Regent Street, St. James's, London SW1Y 4LR, *tel* +44 (0)20 7393 4400, *fax* +44 (0)20 7393 4401, *email* cb@curtisbrown.co.uk

No performance of any kind may be given unless a licence has been obtained. Applications should be made before rehearsals begin. Publication of this play does not necessarily indicate its availability for amateur performance.

www.nickhernbooks.co.uk/environmental-policy

Nick Hern Books' authorised representative in the EU is
Easy Access System Europe – Mustamäe tee 50, 10621 Tallinn, Estonia
email gpsr.requests@easproject.com

Backstroke was first performed at the Donmar Warehouse, London, on 15 February 2025, with the following cast:

BO	Tamsin Greig
BETH	Celia Imrie
CAROL	Lucy Briers
JILL	Anita Reynolds
PAULINA	Georgina Rich
SKYLAR (*film and stage*)	Chloe Hart
SKYLAR (*stage*)	Tamilore Lawson
TED	Rhashan Stone
Writer and Director	Anna Mackmin
Designer	Lez Brotherston
Lighting Designer	Paule Constable
Sound Designer	Christopher Shutt
Video Designer	Gino Ricardo Green
Casting Director	Anna Cooper CDG
Associate Director	Fiona Dunn
Choreographer	Scarlett Mackmin
Film Producer	Richard Holmes
Cinematographer	Damian Paul Daniel
Film Line Producer	Sarah Boyks
Production Manager (Stage)	David Pritchard
Company Stage Manager	Caoimhe Regan
Deputy Stage Manager	Caitlin Shay
Assistant Stage Manager	Jamie Craker
Stage Management Intern	Tashi Dema
Costume Supervisor	Hattie Barsby
Props Supervisor	Laura Flowers
Video Programmer	Daberechi Ukoha-Kalu
Production Photographer	Johan Persson

SHORT FILM CREW

1st Assistant Director	Gareth Tandy
2nd Assistant Director	Chloe Andrews
Film Production Manager	Stephanie Faucher
Underwater Choreography	Scarlett Mackmin
Stunt Coordinator	Maisie Carter
Hair & Make-Up Artist	Rosemary Williams
Art Department	Laura Flowers
Art Department Assistant	Hannah Rawson
Art Department Assistant	Lucie Brooks Butler
Film Costume Assistant	Lucy Griffiths
Location Manager	Tom Clarke
Location Marshall	Fin Graham
Production Runner/Driver	Emily Roberts
Assistant Director Runner	Ollie Pitman
1st Assistant Camera	Arie Priebe
2nd Assistant Camera	Jonathan Boyd
Gaffer	Kevin Gardner
Underwater Gaffer	Kevan Noble
Sound Recordist	Pierluigi Papaiz
Boom Operator	George Blake
Celia Double/ Underwater Swimmer	Kate Giles
Tamsin Double/ Underwater Swimmer	Hillary Liesching
Underwater Camera Tech	Ross Birnie
Water Safety/Camera Assistant	Marti Guiver
Additional Underwater Photography	Rosie Taylor

Acknowledgements

Anna Mackmin would like to thank Stephen Russell, Scarlett Mackmin, Grant Parsons, Timothy Sheader, Lez Brotherston and Imogen Brodie. There'd be no *Backstroke* without you.

Sincere gratitude to the company: Tamsin Greig, Celia Imrie, Georgina Rich, Lucy Briers, Anita Reynolds, Chloe Hart and Rhashan Stone. Thanks to the creative team: Paule Constable, Gino Ricardo Green, Christopher Shutt, Fiona Dunn, Damian Paul Daniel, Richard Holmes, Laura Flowers and Hattie Barsby. Never forgetting the incomparable stage management of: Caoimhe Regan, Caitlin Shay and Jamie Craker. Thanks too, to *Backstroke*'s first readers: Amelia Bullmore, Niamh Cusack, Giselle Glasman, Deena Gornick, Rebecca Lyon, Lisa Makin and Kate Reich. Thank you to Nicola Walker and Sheila Hancock for setting us on our way. Thanks to the film team and to everyone at the Donmar involved in the making of *Backstroke* – your relentless graft has been hugely appreciated. And, to the mothers of all these people, living and dead, thank you, you raised some exceptional humans.

Ronnie.
This play isn't about you but it is for you.
Thank you, darling.

Characters

BETH, *early twenties to mid-seventies*
BO, *five to fifty-one*
JILL, *fifties*
CAROL, *fifties*
PAULINA, *forties*
LENGTHS SWIMMER, *fifties, on film only*
PARAMEDIC ONE, *fifties*
PARAMEDIC TWO, *fifties*
PARAMEDIC THREE, *fifties*
KELLY GREEN, *funeral director, fifties*
TED, *fifties, on film only*
SKYLAR, *eight*

Note on Text

Forward slashes (/) at the end, and start, of a line indicate speech should be interrupted.

Bold text indicates a filmed sequence, to be projected above Bo's head. They reveal her, mostly, immediate memories.

The action runs seamlessly from scene to scene.

This text went to press before the end of rehearsals and so may differ slightly from the play as performed.

ACT ONE

Scene One

The set's part-kitchen, part-hospital. The back wall's used to project film on. The action runs seamlessly.

A hospital emergency, underscored by music, distorted as if underwater. **On film: a car hurtling down a country lane. We hear Bo: 'I have to get there so I can get back.' Film out.**

Lights up on a hospital bed, containing a vacant and still BETH *(seventies).* BETH *has filthy hair and nightwear.* BO *(fifty-one) enters.*

BO. Beth?

> BO *studies her dying mother, sniffs her, contemplates touching her mother's face. Can't. Sits.*
>
> *Above* BO, **film flicks into life, it shows a memory of last night.**
>
> **Bo's bedroom. Night.**
>
> **Bo at home in bed with Ted, her sleeping husband. Bo's awake. Skylar (Bo and Ted's child) calls, terrified, from a different room.**

SKYLAR. Come, come, come!

> **Bo shoots upright.**
>
> *On stage,* BO *stands.*
>
> **Sound and film out.**
>
> BO *fires into action, removing disintegrating clothes from a bag.*

I'm not tidying you up. I'm going to wash these, they…

The dress BO*'s holding is so decayed it looks like lace.* BO*'s halted.*

Christ!

She shoves it in the bag. It's horrible and BO *is scared.*

Your clothes are made of holes. Your clothes, Beth. They're useless.

PAULINA (*consultant*), CAROL (*nurse*) *enter.*

PAULINA. Good morning. How're we getting on in here? I'm Paulina Markham, consultant.

BO *jumps, semi-hides her bag.*

BO. Yes, hello, hi, I remember, hello…

PAULINA. And, this is…

BO. Yes. Hi…

PAULINA. Carol.

BO. Yes, come in, bit cosy but obviously thank you for the room, it's…

PAULINA. Space, we have a little more of that than a London hospital.

BO. Yes.

PAULINA. Well. We'd like to do some tests, then Carol here would like to give, what's that, Carol?

CAROL. Yogurt. You love your yogurt, don't you, Beth?

PAULINA. How are you doing, Bethan? I see here you are seventy-six, is that correct, Bethan? You are seventy-six years of age? Are you making sure she's getting all the liquids you can /

BO. / I don't want to be rude but, sorry, she doesn't like yogurt.

CAROL. She likes her cherry.

PAULINA. Thank you, Carol. What about liquids?

ACT ONE, SCENE ONE 13

BO. Sorry but she doesn't.

PAULINA. And what about liquids?

CAROL. She had a nice little go of cherry in the night, gave me such a lovely thank-you smile for it too.

BO. She doesn't like yogurt, sorry. She hates cherry, and, sorry, I'm not sure how much she wants liquids.

PAULINA. It's important she gets them.

BO. Okay. But.

PAULINA. Bethan? Hello? Bethan?

BO. Beth.

PAULINA. Thank you. Beth? I'm Paulina Markham, I'm a consultant here at the Community Hospital, we met briefly when you were admitted. Beth? I'd like you to tell me who this is?

Indicates BO. *Nothing from* BETH.

Who is this? Can you say her name? What's her name?

Nothing.

Tell me who this is?

Nothing.

BO. She has no idea who I am.

PAULINA. This is your daughter, Beth. What's her name?

BETH. Bh, Bh.

PAULINA. Good.

BO. What?!

PAULINA. Thank you, Beth, we're now going to take a small amount of blood. We will do our best to make it as painless as possible. Carol?

CAROL *takes blood, it causes* BETH *discomfort and worry.*

BO. Just a sec, what's it for? Sorry, can you tell me?

PAULINA. Beth's been showing some surprising shifts. It appeared, on admission, she quite possibly only had a few /

BO. / Do you mind if? (*Gesturing to the doorway.*) I know she probably can't hear, or isn't registering but, could we?

BO and PAULINA clump in the doorway. CAROL stays.

PAULINA. The results of the scan have come back, Beth's stroke was surprisingly, impressively, small.

BO. Impressively?

PAULINA. It can happen, this temporary paralysis of what you might think of as personality, even in dementia patients, the brain readjusts to /

BO. / She's not dying?

PAULINA. With the right care she could live for /

BO. / But? Right. So not a few weeks?

PAULINA. We all do this differently, she might fall for a further stroke tomorrow.

BO. Fall? What about the drip?

PAULINA. She's getting everything she needs from it? And, possibly more critically, we can administer pain relief via it. Her notes say she suffers from sciatica.

BO. Not for years. Where did that come from? Do her notes say anything about her agoraphobia? Her hypochondria?

PAULINA. She has had a stroke. Do we have notes about these other conditions?

BO. I don't know. All her illness is real but I don't know if the causes are.

PAULINA. What we're looking at is her current condition, looking into causes might not /

BO. / When my perimenopausal symptoms started, Beth began pouring with sweat. She was seventy. I am aware I might

ACT ONE, SCENE ONE 15

sound cruel and she doesn't have an advance directive, or anything useful but, I am, I'm trying to...

PAULINA. Has she got an advance directive? She has had a stroke.

BO. No, I said, nothing, not even a will, but, I do know. She doesn't want feeding. Or anything. Okay? Please can we take it out?

PAULINA. If we take it out she might not get enough liquid, that can be painful and, as I said, the drip can also be the swiftest way to administer pain relief.

BO. If she's not dying, and of course she mustn't be in pain, I want her to be able to choose. Choose. Or, sorry, not.

PAULINA. Do we have notes about, forgive me, what name do you like to use?

BO. Bo's fine. Sorry, they did say, everyone was clear, last night, on admission, that she was...

PAULINA. It would be enormously useful, Bo, if she had drawn up an advance directive. I think under the circumstances /

BO. / I did try. When will you know if she's dying? Or can't you? She hasn't been like that with me, that name-sound.

PAULINA. Sometimes patients manifest more active behaviour around strangers.

BO. You don't think she's dying.

PAULINA. Do we understand correctly that independent care, or caring for her at home /

BO. / I live in London. The man my mother's married to, Dominic, can't do any more. I did try to set up help. But she wouldn't, she gets, it's fear.

PAULINA. Your father will have needed support.

BO. He's not my father and I do understand that, I did try but, I can't have her with me. I'm sorry, but I can't.

PAULINA. The social work team can provide you with a list of appropriate residential homes. It can be a confusing time.

BO. Not a home. Sorry, but I can't. Would you move her with the drip?

PAULINA. You must remember, it is early days. We'll get someone to call you.

BO. Will you take it out first? Please? See how she is then? And, sorry but, I don't want to be rude, but can you say she's not to be force-fed?

PAULINA. No one working here would force-feed. You can say anything you need directly to the nursing team.

The medics are leaving. BO *calls after them.*

BO. I mean not put stuff in her mouth. Sorry. Can food and drink be placed for her to take if she wants? Or not. I know how I must sound, but she, I just can't.

Film into life.

Bo's bedroom. A different night.

Bo at home in bed with Ted, her sleeping husband. Bo's awake. Skylar calls, terrified, from a different room.

SKYLAR. Come, come, come!!!

Bo shoots upright.

On stage, BO *exits, fast.*

Film out.

Scene Two

On stage. Hospital. Pre-dawn. Sound of distant hospital.

BETH (*seventies*) *alone.* JILL *enters.*

JILL. Morning, Beth.

Checks BETH, *opens curtains, offers water,* BETH's *unmoving.*

I'll pop back later, lovely.

JILL *leaves.*

BO *enters, hovers. Sits.*

BO. Sorry I can't get here every day.

BO *watches* BETH. *No connection.* BO *gets out her mobile, moves to the doorway. Dials.*

Ted, hi, it's me. Obviously it's me. I'm really sorry to have to ask, I know you've had to collect Skylar again and you were supposed to be taking your Year Ten lot on that thing and sorry but if you get a moment please can you look up care homes? Near us. I know we've no spare money and I don't know what the hell it'll cost or, how would we even get her there? They keep saying I have to find somewhere. I think there's no way I can, we can, and Dominic comes for forty minutes every other day and I know I do less but I, she is. I miss you. Please let me know how Skylar is. You know the worst? She smells. Like a huge version of like my head smells, if I don't wash my hair. Sorry. And sorry I'm sometimes smelly. I will try not to be. Thank you. Even if you don't manage to find a care home. But please do. Bye. Bye.

BO *moves back.* BETH *groans.*

Beth?

Nothing.

Water?

Film up.

Skylar's bedroom. Night. A hand-made-by-Beth rug. Skylar's being carried and joggled. Bo's lull-singing 'When You Smile' by Shirley Bassey. Ted's holding a night-light. Skylar's too big to be rocked to sleep.

Bo inches Skylar down to the bed. Ted begins to stand. Skylar snaps awake, begins thrashing to escape.

Ted! She was asleep! Why can't you judge these things?!

Skylar's kicking out.

Ow, oo, ouch! Stop! Please! We're not a hurting family!

Film out.

So.

Nothing.

Skylar's managing to stay at school at least an hour some days. You were right, she can do it. The teachers say she's clever. Don't know where they get that from, she's never there. But, right again. Beth?

Nothing.

So. You might like this. We were cooking. It's something I can do with her, partly just filling in hours but I suppose also, I'm trying to teach her she's home. She was sitting sideways on the work surface with that recipe book you made when I was about her age. I was studying her, I never get to just look at her, we have to carry her everywhere – no doubt why she panics at school, got to stand on her own two feet.

Nothing.

BO *goes to the window, opens it. Breathes.*

She spoke. It was her voice, but not, she sounded like a fifty-year-old well-fed Tory – 'I think we might find you've forgotten the vanilla.' She can't properly read. Especially not your handwriting, but, it was freaky, she was fluent – 'Chocolate idiot biscuits, so called because they're so simple even an idiot can make them.'

Closes the window.

She's like her granny, I know, I know, I'm not supposed to call you granny, but she is. How's that possible?

BETH. Bh… Bh.

BO. Me? Bo? My name?

BETH. Bph.

BO. Oh. Beth.

BO *leaves the hospital.*

Scene Three

It's a new day. BETH*'s alone, the position of the drip's causing discomfort.*

BO *enters on stage, bringing **the film up.***

Bo in car, early morning, barrelling along, light blurs past. The radio's on loud. Bo's singing manically to 'Uptown Funk' by Mark Ronson ft. Bruno Mars.

Film out.

BO *stands with her back to* BETH. BETH*'s leg's snaking with pain.* BETH *stretches to* BO. BO*'s oblivious.* BETH *gives up.* JILL *enters.* BO *spins.*

JILL. Morning, Beth. How we doing, my lovely? Morning.

BO. Morning.

JILL *to the water jug, then to* BETH *with water.*

I can do that. Let me.

JILL (*not handing it over*). How much have you given her today?

BO. She never seems to want it.

JILL. Course she does. She can't say, everybody needs water. Come on, lovely, here we go. That's good, isn't it? There.

JILL's raised BETH's head, and got water into her mouth. BETH barely registers.

BO. Please, let me. Here. I'll take that.

BO takes the cup. JILL into action.

JILL. I need to take Mum's blood pressure. That alright with you?

BO. Yes, of course. Shall I stay?

JILL. It's only her blood pressure, why wouldn't you?

BO. Yes. Thank you.

JILL. You're welcome.

JILL wraps the pressure gauge. BETH winces, cries.

Oh! It's alright, it's very quick, it's just the pressure thing, it'll be over soon. Oh!

Good. Well, that's all fine. All done, Beth, alright, my lovely?

BO's close to BETH's head. BETH grabs her arm. JILL watches. BO tries to soothe BETH, without touching her.

BO. It's done now. Okay. Do you want some water?

Smallest nod from BETH.

JILL. There, what a good girl. That's right, Beth, your daughter's here and she's going to give you some water. Just lift her head. Go on. Tilt it right up.

BO braces, lifts her mother's head, attempts to give water. It dribbles.

BO. Oh!

JILL. That's alright. You got some in. I'll mop that. You get another wee sip in. There. That's better isn't it, lovely?

JILL's *mopping*, BO's *re-tilting the glass*. CAROL *enters*.

CAROL. I hear you want the drip taken out?

BO. Yes, but only if the doctors say so. Do they say it's alright to?

JILL (*to* CAROL). Are you doing it?

CAROL. She wants it taken out.

BO. When did they decide to do it? Are you doing it?

CAROL. I've been told I've got to.

BO. Are they moving her?

JILL. Where'd you get that from? They can't move her until you say. Have you found somewhere?

CAROL. For goodness' sake. They can't move her! Look at her.

BO. They said she wasn't... They, the consultant, said she wasn't... Sorry, can we?

BO *gestures to the semi-privacy of the doorway. They clump there.*

I really truly promise I'm not trying to, but, can you tell me? You must have seen this so many times. Do you think she's...?

CAROL. She's very, very ill is how she is, which is why it's cruel to take this drip out.

JILL. Carol, love.

CAROL. I won't be party to hurrying someone along or causing pain, we have a duty of care, and there's all those nights when you 'can't' be here, can you? Water won't keep her alive. Not even giving her a little something to comfort her.

BO. No one is asking that. All I've ever asked is – if she is well enough to move to a care home, she's well enough to choose if she eats, or drinks.

CAROL. And you've demanded we take it out.

BO. No. Not demanded anything.

CAROL. But you want it out?

BO. Yes, but /

CAROL. / There, that's exactly what I'm saying.

BO. She never wrote it down but she said it over and over and now she's like this and before this, she's so far down the road with /

CAROL. / Dementia patients can live for years. Quite happily. I won't be party to this. Who are /

BO. / It's about choice. Her choice.

CAROL. That's your job now, how can /

JILL. / Carol, love, step outside. Come on. Now. Come on.

JILL, with an arm round CAROL, leads her out.

Film up.

Bo's bedroom. A different night.

Bo in bed with Ted who's asleep. Bo's awake. Skylar calls terrified from a different room.

SKYLAR. Come, come, come!!!

JILL back in.

Film out.

JILL. Sorry about that. She takes it personally. We have said to her it might feel different, when she's had her own mother like this. You can't know until it's happened to you.

BO. She shouldn't be allowed /

JILL. / She's a good nurse. Right. Let's get this out.

JILL starts drip removal. BETH whimpers, clutching at BO.

BO. No, no, no.

JILL. It's ever so quick. Nearly done.

BO. Nearly done. Well done. You're being so brave.

JILL. There. Done.

JILL's stroking BETH *with ease.* BETH *calms.*

She can stay here you know.

BO. What do you mean? How long can she stay?

JILL. Until. They can't move her unless you've found somewhere and if you don't find somewhere or agree to their choice, well.

BO. Do you think she's...?

JILL. Yes, love.

BO's phone rings.

BO. This is, it's my child's school, I've got to...

BO *moves to the doorway.* JILL *leaves.*

Hello?... Did she?! *So* sorry... I do have to apologise... I'm three hours away, please don't tell her that, please tell her, her dad might be an hour or so but he will come.

BO *buttons her phone, leaves the room, punch-dialling Ted's number.* BO*'s speaking, travelling down the corridor.*

Ted, it's me. School have called, I know this is the worst possible timing but please can you...

Sound of the hospital swirls around BETH. *Unmoving.*
CAROL *enters, carrying yogurt.*

CAROL. Look what I've saved off the trolley for your din-dins. Let's get you sat up.

CAROL*'s pager beeps.*

No rest for the wicked! You hold tight, I'll be right back.

CAROL *picks up the yogurt and moves to go, passing* BO, *who's returning.* BO *gestures to her phone.*

BO. I've got to...

CAROL *blanks her and exits.* BO *grabs her things, rushing to leave, then pauses. Might this be the last time* BO *sees her mother alive?*

Um? Goodbye. I suppose.

Nothing.

School have called. I have to go. Bye, Beth. Beth? Mummy?

Nothing.

BO *doesn't leave. Waits to see if calling* BETH *'Mummy' will register.*

Scene Four

The opening bars of Shirley Bassey's 'When You Smile', but far away and underwater. BETH *sits up.*

BETH. Mummy?! How many times? I have a name, please use it.

BETH (*sixties*) *swings lovely legs from the bed, she's shedding years, she stands, finds a wrap, ties it over ragged nightclothes, steps from hospital into her kitchen, sits in a chair draped with a shawl and lights a cigarette.*

Egg?! Darling?!

BETH *smokes.*

Darling?! One mother fading to nothing in here!

BO (*forties*) *collects a bin bag and papers from the hospital cupboard, steps into the kitchen.*

BO. If you want my help with this – god sorry but – all this rubbish, then please can you do the egg?

BETH. I wasn't asking you to 'do' the eggs, plural, I was asking how you'd like yours cooked. Don't be so fucking tetchy. I have to get on top of my filing. Apparently, I'm required to

get things straightened out, to discern whether I might
qualify for some sort of – bleugh – pension. A pension!?
How has that come to pass?

BO. You're sixty-four. It's normal for women when they hit
sixty to claim a pension. If they've paid any tax.

BETH. Must you always drag things down to the miserable
particulars?! Sixty-four, forty-six, where's the difference?

BO. Weell…

BETH. I'm still me! Can you not just be a darling and help?
You know I'd do the egg myself in a wink but I'm crippled
by this bastard of a leg.

BETH *attempts to stand*.

BO. Okay, sit still, it's fine.

BO *cooks plus surreptitious cleaning*. BETH *writes in
a yellow notebook*.

BETH. When was the last time I took my medication?

BO. Why?

BETH. I have to record every single thing I take. For the doctor.
Truly wonderful, you know, at the? Yes, doctors. New
doctor. Really thinks he can sort my bastard leg and even do
something for my head. I call him, what do I call him?

BO. I don't know. You could ask Dominic.

BETH. Not that dreary arsehole.

BO. No.

BETH. Doctor Spock! I told him Spock was my bible with you.
And this one, conveniently, has remarkably sharp ears.

BO. Not to his face?

BETH (*preparing paracetamol*). But of course. He was charmed.

BO (*handing food*). I thought you hadn't had a migraine for
a year or so.

BETH. Pop those scrambles on the side, I'll make a pass at them later. Must just get this para-thingy down. Date?

BO. October twenty-second.

BETH *drops paracetamol, begins furious scribbling in the notebook.*

Don't forget to take the pill before you write it down.

BETH. Christ on his perilous and hairy bike, you can be rude! Memory's not the problem. My leg is the problem. And my head. And sometimes, on a truly horrid day, the endless shitting.

BO*'s ripping up bank statements.*

Pen! If you will insist on this relentless tidying of me, you need to scribble through the address and, the, bits, you have to remove all, surely I told you?

BO. These statements are over twelve years out of date. The account doesn't exist, the tax person has no use for them, they're rubbish.

BETH. I see those statements as a kind of postscriptum to my creative achievements. My Life Upon the Loom.

BO. I'm not being rude but your woven sculptures haven't put you above the tax threshold for the last thirty years.

BETH. What about the fortune I've amassed from my work with property?

BO. Living in houses isn't work.

BETH. Living in this house with Dominic has been fucking hard work.

BO. Fair dos.

BETH. Come closer, that miserable sod categorically refuses to let me draw up a bill.

BO. What for?

BETH. The future.

BO. What are you planning?

BETH. Death.

BO. When?

BETH. Fuck's sake, must you? I don't bloody know. I plan on many, preferably glorious years. Did I tell you? I think my next project will be an eco-house.

BO. Is that what the bill's for?

BETH. What blasted bill? Who's charging?

BO. You said, Dominic's being tight about some bill.

BETH. You really must get your ears syringed. I said, will.

BO. You've done one. I got you one of those easy ones from the Post Office. Years ago.

BETH. He burnt it. Made a pyre and howled with laughter as it went up. Whoosh!

BO. Right.

BETH. I'd left it all to you. Argh! Leg! Bollocking, bastard, leg!

BO. You are married.

BETH. I'm not sure we believe in marriage, do we?

BO. You didn't use to but, things change.

BETH. Only if you make them change. Only if you work insanely hard, sacrifice, categorically refuse, why do people say refuse instead of rubbish? When did that commence?

BO. God knows. Shall I corner Dominic about the whereabouts of your will?

BETH. Dominic is never home from the bookshop before lights-out. Do you think you could be an angel and knock me up a little something eggy on toast?

BO. Sure.

BO pretends to cook again. BETH writes.

BETH. So, absolutely gorgeous new doctor. Reminded me of your father, dear Anthony of the silken sheath. You know? Think it was the doc's ears that prompted this train of thought. Anyroad. Whenever your daddy went down on me I used to have the same fantasy. About a hare. Rabbit kind not the barnet type. I'd be holding on to its endless velvety ears, caressing, mmm, whilst it worried away at my dillypot, digging its sharp little claws into my thighs, then, when I came, it would look up with its beady perceptive eyes and lick its raspy wee lips. Heaven. It was all I could think of with this doctor. Doctor? Spock! Because of the ears. *Naturellement.*

BO (*re-presenting eggs*). Sounds like Dominic's missing a trick.

BETH. Oh, he gave up fucking about two years, sorry months, after he finally trapped me. How thoughtful. My absolute favourite. You're a good girl when you try. Will you have some?

BETH *gives* BO *a hard stare.*

No. Best not.

She taps her thighs significantly, with a look to BO's *thighs.*

BO. Careful of the leg.

BETH *raises an eyebrow, tucks in.*

BETH. Pass my ciggies, will you.

She lights up.

BO. That is the single most disgusting habit left over from seventies communal living. Smoking whilst eating.

BETH. Don't be such a priss. Little bit of seventies gung-ho is exactly what you're missing.

BO. Gung-ho stems from the Chinese word for working together, did you know? Not sure – but if one were being pedantic /

BETH. / And why change the habit of a lifetime? /

BETH *back to her writing.*

ACT ONE, SCENE FOUR 29

BO. / Not sure, if *work* was what you were up to, in the famous seventies. Wasn't it just hare-related activities? The bonds of marriage swapped for the bonds of free love?

BETH. I suppose it might be obstinacy, this addiction you've fostered to missing the point.

BO. Which is?

BETH. Love.

BO. Not – ensnaring a man, keeping him enthralled, but mostly just keeping him, your protection against the big scary world?

BETH. That, my cyclical, ha, wrong word but isn't the brain a marvellous thing? My *cynical* darling – what you're describing would be prostitution.

BETH *hasn't looked up from her opus and appears to have forgotten to smoke her cigarette.* BO *stubs it. Pushes eggs towards* BETH. BETH *pushes them back.*

Don't assume, because I am creatively engaged, I won't notice if you snaffle my lunch.

BO. You're writing a list.

BETH. I often think poetry is merely list-writing, masquerading as art.

BO *checks if she's being witnessed, then chucks bank statements into a bin bag.*

BO. Actually, Beth? I do have something I think you should know. If you're interested?

BETH *stops writing.*

BETH. I am interested in every single thing about you.

BO. I feel a bit silly now.

BETH. Do buck up and stop being such an Effie Lump.

BO. Okay. Well. Ted and I, we are, have, started on the process of adoption. I thought I should tell you.

BETH. Is this some kind of sickly joke?

BO. Possibly. I hope not.

BETH. Do you categorically promise you will never ever un-say that?

BO. Ahrm.

BETH. It will be the making of you. And your Teddy. You are of course chronically ancient but better late.

BO. They don't care how old you are. Apparently, for every four point five kids suitable for adoption there's only one parent slash set of parents available.

BETH. Whatever you do, do not get yourself lumbered with the point five. Just because you're middle-aged they can't make you take the leftovers. Get a beautiful one. I think Chinese mixed with Scandinavian would be exquisite.

BO. They say it might take up to four years.

BETH. Four years?! You'll be nine hundred. Which forty are you again?

BO. Forty!

BETH. Fuck.

BO. What? What fuck? My periods are regular. I could have a biological baby.

BETH. Getting the curse is not the same as being futile.

BO. I'm exceptionally fertile.

BETH. You have to move house! Who else do you have to change nappies whilst you're effing lumping? Move in here! Now, this, is more like it.

BO. Sweet of you but Ted's school, I'm at the studio half the week, I know the Effie Lump only squeaks but I have to write a full script for them to, well actually, for them to dick about and change endlessly but it still has to be done. In London.

BETH. Consider my 'sweet' offer. Do not take this the wrong way but, when I embarked on, you… Christ, you have no idea what is coming.

BO. It's not like when you flirted with adoption and had those Vietnamese twins to stay for the week.

BETH. I had completely forgotten about them. Your almost-brothers. Oh, do come home, it's yours.

BO. Only if you have made a will.

BETH. I can curl up in any old corner. We will raise your little one together, my bastard leg is throbbing.

BETH unties the wrap, steps into hospital, BO *reattaches the catheter.* BETH *lies down. Closes her eyes.*

Watch what you're doing that fucking hurt.

BO. Sorry. School have called, I have to go. Bye, Beth. Beth?

BETH's once again blank. BO *has no choice, she leaves.*

Scene Five

Film up.

Skylar's bedroom. Night.

Skylar's melting down. Bo's attempting to safe-hold. Ted's standing, clutching the bedraggled Effie Lump – a chunkily woven lump with wonky ears, tassel legs and the beak/trunk of a curlew. Skylar's shouting, fighting.

SKYLAR. Take me home, let me go, take me home!

Film out.

New day, underscored by distant sounds of a swimming pool. BO *enters.*

BO. Hello.

Nothing.

Sorry I couldn't get here over the weekend.

BO*'s about to sit when her phone rings.* **Film on.**

What now?!

BO *buttons her phone.*

On stage, BO *moves to doorway.*

On film: the country lay-by. Day.

Bo's pulled over, on her phone, sound of her having a pee behind the open car door.

***The Effie Lump* got cancelled years ago! This is a new idea, any chance we can reschedule?... Not at all?**

Film out.

BO*'s phone rings again. She answers.*

I can't commit to a week's work at the moment, I might be able to do a day... I'm sorry about that but my mother's... Yup, understood.

BO *buttons phone. Steadies her breathing. Moves back.*

Sorry. Hello.

BO *notices* BETH*'s mouth.* BO *exits, fast, returns with* JILL.

Look inside. What's that? All that crustiness. That's food.

JILL *holds* BETH*'s hand.*

See that? That orange-ness. What is that, some custard stuff? I thought we'd said.

JILL. Thrush. It's very common. Why don't you help me clean it out?

BO. Right. Is it sore? It looks /

JILL. / Looks much worse than it is. Poor love.

JILL *prepares.*

Here, come on, Bo, isn't it? You come here and hold this.

JILL *teaches* BO *to wipe* BETH's *cracked and claggy mouth.* BO's *shaking.*

We need that. Here, you have a wee go. Just a gentle wipe. See, it'll come off. There. Easy. Done. Is that better, my lovely? (*Proffers a bin.*) Pop that in here.

BO *drops the cloth in the bin.*

Hands?

They wash together.

Better?

BO. Mm.

They watch BETH.

JILL. Shall we change that nightie?

BO. Oh god yes please! I've no idea where that came from, she'd never wear something like that, even when it was new, she was cripplingly vain. Sorry. I brought something, but I've not seen it on her.

JILL. Let's have a rummage.

JILL *opens bedside cupboard, it's full of bin bags.*

Do you see it?

BO. There, that blue. It's just a T-shirt thing, not really her style, too plain, but it's clean.

JILL. D'you want to do a bit of lip-salve?

BO. No. But thank you.

JILL. You sure? She strikes me as the lippy kind.

BO. Actually, you're so right. Come on /

BETH. / Argh, argh, argh!!

BETH's *raised herself, punching her stomach in pain and panic.*

JILL. Hold her! Hold her tight, gently. Keep her hands down that's it keep holding /

BO. / Oh god oh no oh please what is it?! Help her, please! What is it /

JILL. / I need to get pain relief in quickly. Can you hold her /

BO. / Yes, yes, quickly /

JILL. / Gently. There, Beth love, it's going to be fine. Hold her arms, I'm going to flip her /

BO. / What are you doing?!

JILL. / Over we go /

She turns BETH *onto her side.*

BO. / What are you /

JILL. / Pain relief. Here we go /

BO. / What /

JILL. / Her bottom. It's quickest /

BO. / Yes, right, of course oh dear, no! It's going to work in a second.

BETH*'s crying, clinging to* BO. JILL *tries to insert rectal pain relief.*

JILL. You poor love. She's completely blocked. This'll be painful, I'm very sorry.

BO. Please, please can you, can you get it out?

Time stands still.

JILL. I'm trying. There. That's some of it.

Excruciating pain, horror for BO *and* JILL.

That's as much as I could get. I can't get that pessary in. I'm so sorry. Let's get you back over, lovely. Ready?

They turn BETH *back.* BETH*'s pain subsides.*

I'm nipping to get some pain relief. I'll be back in a second, she seems easier with some of that out, maybe it wasn't the leg, maybe it was her tummy. You alright?

BO *nods*.

Back in a second.

She goes. BO *opens the window. Hot flush.* CAROL *enters, preparing to inject pain relief.* BO *closes window.*

BO. What's that? Where's Jill?

CAROL. Called to an emergency. You've got me. It's pain relief. Quickest we can administer since we no longer have the drip and you've just refused rectal pessaries.

BO. I would never ever, ever, refuse my mother pain relief. That would be monstrous. They, Jill, couldn't get them in. She was too blocked up.

CAROL. I see.

CAROL *injects pain relief.* BETH *clings to* BO.

There you go, Beth. All done. That should start working ever so soon.

CAROL *goes to help* BETH *to a drink*.

Keeping them hydrated helps with down below.

CAROL *exits*.

Film up.

Car/country lane. Day.

Torrential rain. Bo driving, leant forward peering through the windscreen, wipers on fast.

On stage, BO*'s phone beeps. She stabs a reply.* ***Film's wiped away.***

BO. I have to – (*Shakes phone at* BETH.) I'll do my best to get here in the next couple of days.

BO *can't leave. Sits.*

Film up.

Bo's bedroom. Night.

Ted's asleep. Skylar calls, terrified, from her room.

SKYLAR. Come, come, come!!!

On stage, BO *closes her eyes.* ***Film out.*** *Sound of a siren.*

Scene Six

BETH *opens her eyes.* BETH *gets out of bed, tiptoes to* BO. *Whispers.*

BETH. Shift yourself, lazy bones.

> BETH *(forties) steps into kitchen. She finds a handloom, strung with the recognisable beginnings of Skylar's rug. It's a bright day.*
>
> (*Singing to the tune of Joan Baez's 'We Shall Overcome'.*)
> We shall oversleep, we shall oversleep, we shall oversleep, most days. Oh, deep in my heart I do believe…
>
> BETH *makes coffee, lights a cigarette.* BO (*eighteen*) *wakes, collects a bag of belongings and into the kitchen.*

BO. Why didn't you wake me up?

> BETH *contemplates some more.*
>
> Beth? Are you listening to me? Why didn't you wake me up?

BETH. Sorry, darling, did you say something?

BO. Fuck's sake, Beth, I've missed my train!

BETH. You're eighteen, old enough to vote, old enough to flick the switch on your Minnie Mouse alarm. Coffee?

BO. It's broken! You said you'd wake me!

BETH. Don't shout, darling, nothing turns a mouth into a cat's arsehole quicker than mean-spirited yelping.

BO. I've missed my train! You promised!

BETH. But I have woken you. Coffee?

BO. It's nearly nine! I'm going to have to bus and then, oh bloody, bloody hell! I won't get there until tomorrow and I'll miss the signing-in, and for once in my bloody life doing things at the normal time like everyone else and just /

BETH. / I don't suppose for a second you'll be missed. They'll be far too busy eyeing each other up. I remember my first day at university /

BO. / Oh my god, I know! Everyone flocked and couldn't believe your beauty but then, oh dear, two days later you were struck down by some mysterious, simply horrid, something, forcing you to spend the rest of the year in bed, you've told me a million times. You promised me, Beth! I'm going to hitch.

She doesn't. She puts her bag down. BETH *pours coffee, offers a cigarette.* BO *shakes her head.*

BETH. Teeniest bit of advice, darling, if you'll forgive the temerity in my offering it. Do not, whatever you do, allow the Bad Fairy Blame down the chimney. She will fly around in the house of your soul, battering her compellingly pretty wings against whichever locked exit she can find, until her wings are in tatters and she is old. A broken fairy is neither use nor ornament to anyone. Blameful or otherwise. Block up the chimney. Send her packing.

BO. Fairies don't come down chimneys.

BETH. This fairy does.

BO. For fuck's sake, Beth, they don't. That's Father Christmas.

BETH. Do not twist my metaphor. And cleverly avoid the point. Blame, darling, it will batter the glitter from your wings.

BO. I am not blaming. I am stating facts. Fact – the alarm clock is broken. Fact – you ping awake at six every single day. Fact – this is the most important morning of my life.

BETH*'s about to interrupt.*

It is, Beth, for god's sake, it is my life, I have a right to say what is my most important day! Fact – you promised to wake me by the latest at seven. Promised. Fact – you have been tiddling around here in your party-nightie since six and it is now almost nine. Plus, Father Christmas is the one who comes down the chimney.

Takes coffee, goes to add milk.

BETH. Forgive me, darling, I'm forced to say this, but, please relinquish the milk. It's the simplest trick. Black coffee speeds the metabolism, sets the bowels on their trotters, keeps you thin. And, I know that word's forbidden – fat is a feminist issue of course but who gives a monkey's for principles if you're so fat people can't squeeze past to hear you preach. You'll thank me in the long run. Milky coffee? Well...

BO *adds milk to her coffee, turns away, gathers herself, speaks back into the room.*

BO. D'you need to come with me?

BETH. How funny, I had been wondering whether I might be useful to you, do all the boring legwork, find us some digs, whilst you were busy being clever.

BO. Us?

BETH. Not forever, don't be silly, just until.

BO. Yup. How would you manage that legwork? I'd be in lectures. Who'd hold your hand?

BETH. I'd find someone, never you fear. It might be fun. Promise I wouldn't cramp, I did miss out on so much, when I should have been larking around at university, this might be a chance for me to relive some of my youth. Don't make that face. I'd only bring this little travelling loom and a few things, honestly, if you would only listen to me about the dairy you could squeeze into my frocks. We could share! Taxi? My treat?

BO. It's three hundred miles.

BO turns. BETH drops eye contact. Her hands are shaking as she lights another cigarette.

BETH. Please.

BO. You can cope on your own. I know you can. I'm sorry but, please will you understand? I am going to hitch. Beth?

BETH won't look at her. Her breathing's speeding up.

I'm going to hitch. I am going to go. I have to. Please say goodbye. Please.

BETH's shaking too much to smoke. Her breathing's too fast, too high in her chest.

Please will you say goodbye?

BETH. I can't do it.

BO. You can. You have so many friends. And what's-his-name, he'll come running, 'specially if you call him round now, put the party-nightie to use, but please, Beth, please will you try to go it alone? Just for five minutes? Try not to call him?

BETH's rocking.

I'm going to go now. I have to. So, bye. Please say goodbye. Please.

Nothing.

Alright then. Bye.

BO exits, the front door opens and closes.

BETH is alone.

The front door opens. BO walks back into the kitchen.

BETH. Hello, darling, did you forget something?

BO. I'm going to call what's-his-name? Dominic. And if he can't come and look after you then, okay, you can come but, I'm bringing you home at the weekend. Regardless.

Film up.

Day. Bo's kitchen.

Bo (fifty-one), with too-big Skylar on her lap. Bo's laptop open. Skylar thumps her head, backwards against Bo's chest. Bo raises a hand, to shield her face in case Skylar bangs her again.

This is Mummy's work! Find the part of you that's calm and use that part to...

Skylar crashes hands down on the computer keyboard. On stage, BO *leads* BETH, *shaking, to the bed.* BETH *closes her eyes. Film out.*

I have to go.

BO *leaves*.

Scene Seven

CAROL *enters*.

CAROL. Morning, Beth, here, look what I've got here – all clean.

Brandishes Beth's hairbrush. Brushes.

'And even the very hairs of your head are all numbered. Fear not, therefore you are of more value than many sparrows.'

BO *enters*.

BO. Oh. Hello. Sorry, sorry I couldn't get here yesterday. Thank you, she looks, thank you.

CAROL. Beautiful. I'll pop in and see you later, Beth.

BO. No, you can stay. No need to go.

CAROL. I've got ward rounds, meds to make up, reports.

BO. Of course, well, double thanks then.

CAROL. Right, Beth, I'm off to do my actual job.

CAROL leaves. BETH doesn't register BO. BO opens window, sucks in cool air, unpacks a T-shirt nightie, hovers, sits.

BO. Hello.

Nothing.

Water?

BO tilts the glass. BETH's mouth's closed.

Okay.

BO sneaks a look at her mobile.

(*Under breath.*) Shit on a brick.

Punches a message.

Sorry, um, yes, actually you might be pleased. I did some work. Not finished but it's a start. No one wants to read it but I did manage to write something. This is, remarkably, this is work.

Waves her phone.

I'll button it. It's rubbish anyway. My brain's fried. Sorry. You know what I mean. I will do my best to be alright. You know?

Film up.

Bo's kitchen table. Night.

Bo and Ted sat over their kitchen table, empty glasses and an unopened bottle of red. Bo rests her head on the table. Ted tries to lay his hand on her, she tilts her head, he removes his hand.

Film out.

And, um, Skylar? Your granddaughter?

Nothing.

I was going to try and say things I thought you might need to hear but it's too hard. I can't promise I'm going to be able to cope, just because you might need to feel released or... I think about giving her back. Sorry but I do, and I feel sick even just saying it but I do.

Nothing.

Beth?

Film up.

Swimming pool. Day.

Bo's in the shallow end, Skylar on her hip, Skylar's swathed in armbands, rubber ring, noodle tied above that. Skylar has Bo's shoulders in a pincer grip, pushing up, attempting to get as much of her body free of the water as possible.

SKYLAR. No, no, no, no, no!

BO. I categorically promise the water will hold you. I will hold you.

Film out.

Right. Let's get some food into you then.

BO *leaves*, BETH *doesn't move*. BO *back with a plastic tub of jelly.*

Ta-dah! Lunch.

BO *does her best to spoon food in*. BETH *refuses to open her mouth.*

Bloody, bloody hell.

BO *shoves food in bin.*

Film up.

A field. Night.

Bo's near her parked car, standing in the middle of the field. The sky's swirling with indigo clouds. Bo's staring at the moon.

BETH *hops out of bed, and into the kitchen.*

BO *turns to watch* BETH. ***Film out.***

Scene Eight

BETH *(fifties) is putting finishing touches to an elaborate wildflower garland. She places it on her head. Checks herself in the mirror. Gorgeous. Picks up a yellow notebook, ticks headgear off her list.* BO *speaks from the hospital.*

BO. Seriously? That is your look? *Lord of the Rings* Elven queen?

> BO *(thirties) finds a small, black hat plus veil. Puts it on, enters kitchen.*

BETH. Would you like to borrow some lipstick?

BO. You are fifty-three! You can not skip up to the registry office decked out like that. Sorry but you can't.

BETH. Nobody will be skipping, Dominic has arranged a Gypsy with a pony and trap to collect us.

BO. Please, please do not, whatever you do, call whoever is driving this trap a Gypsy! They are Travellers, travelling people. Oh my god, seriously?! A pony and trap? Why?!

BETH. Because, I have no desire to rock up to the most important day of my life in a Honda Civic with its passenger door secured using gardener's twine. Although blessings on you, for the offer of a lift.

BO. But a trap?!

BETH. Think yourself lucky I chose to downscale Dominic's original, Lady Godiva fantasy. I've spared you the trauma of riding pillion with me through the village.

BO. I'm taking up prayer. For rain.

BETH. Never fear, I am, as ever, leaps ahead of you. I've fashioned an umbrella contraption, for just such an eventuality. It's rather a lovely thing, bedecked with pompoms, and bells.

BO *sits, bows her head.* BETH *gathers a small posy.*

BO. How many bells?

BETH. I lost count, it took three nights to sew them all on.

BETH *proffers the posy, plus hair clips.*

Off with the funereal headgear, darling, let's attach this.

BO *shakes her bowed head.* BETH *makes to remove the hat.*

BO. Do not touch me!

BETH. Now you listen to me, young lady, it's my wedding and I am in charge, whether you like it or not, of appearances. Remove that nasty little suburban-tub affair and pin these, in its place.

BO. Have you got any painkillers?

BO *looks up.*

My period. It was late, really late. I'm bleeding quite heavily.

BETH *pushes the kettle onto the hot plate, leaves the room.* BO*'s in pain.* BETH *returns with painkillers and a hot-water bottle. Fills the bottle. Hands it over. Oblivious to* BO *having been pregnant.*

BETH. The time is now seven forty-five. The wedding breakfast is in one hour. Pull yourself together and let's hear your speech. Clearly I need to vet before we inflict it on the assembled guests.

BO. I'm not doing a speech. I can't. In all conscience. I did try to write one. I'll read a poem. Or something. And I'm not going in your trap. I'll drive and meet you there. Thank you for the hot-water bottle.

BETH. I do not accept this. You will write a speech. And in it you will say how magnificent it is I have finally found my soul's companion and /

BO. / I cannot and I will not accept that the man who runs the bargain basement bookshop whose speciality is porn, masquerading as art-house photography, is the love of your life. He's marrying you because you own a house. You're marrying him because you've finally had to accept I'm never coming back to look after you.

BETH. I hope one day you'll recall this torrent of putrid jealousy and repent. Dominic lays himself naked at my feet every single night to whisper his devotion to his alabaster muse.

BO. Which would explain the foot-fetish shelf at the back of the shop.

BETH. I am his muse! Do you have any idea how many photographs he has taken of me? *All* of me?! Not just my feet.

BO. But not one of them framed and hung in a gallery. What does he do with them?

BETH. You aren't the only artist in this family struggling with recognition.

BO. He is not family!

BETH. He is my family and it is the greatest sorrow of my life not to have been able to produce children for him to father.

BO. What?!

BETH. Just because you're too cowardly to contemplate the inevitable dilution of self mothering requires, does not mean I don't yearn for it hourly.

BO *presses on her aching empty womb.*

BO. I can't be a mother.

BETH. Don't be so melodramatic.

BO. And you already are one. Of sorts.

BETH. Jesus fucking Christ almighty!

BO. There are so many things I never tell you, what would be the point?

BETH. It's what a person doesn't voice that niggles. Regrets, you fool, are like uncut diamonds, grey and jagged, strung on a choker, biting into your throat.

BO. I can't be a mother! /

BETH. / Stop it, you silly, silly girl, not today, do you hear?! /

BO. / When would be a convenient time to talk about something other than you?

BETH. It's my wedding day, you selfish little, only not so fucking little, unfortunately /

BO. / Look at me! Not sideways! See this? My utterly normal body? It's no longer available for you to project your Victorian bullshit ideals of womanhood onto. My body is nothing to do with you!

BETH. Three and a half days in labour. My perineum split to my anus. Nipples grated raw. You *are* me!

The steam of the argument's released. BO's in pain. She's quiet, factual now.

BO. I can't be a mother.

BETH *remains livid*.

BETH. We know that isn't true, I still have a three-hundred-pound hole in my bank account to prove it.

BO *storms from the kitchen*.

Film up.

Car. Day. A grey goose almost collides with the windscreen, flaps sideways, leads Bo along the road.

Come back here!

Film out.

BETH *rushes after* BO. *The front door slams.*

Film in. It plays above the empty stage.

Lay-by. Day.

Bo on her phone out of her car, panic.

BO. Please get out of the staff room and call me, the assessment, social no therapist woman called, they say, she says, it's not just attachment, poor Skylar, it's post-traumatic stress disorder. Like a little baby soldier.

Film out.

Sound of waves, wing beats and underwater echoes of 'When You Smile'.

Above the hospital, the back wall splits horizontally to reveal BO (*thirteen*) *leading* BETH (*thirties*), *step by step onto a beach. Sound reverts to beach.*

Scene Nine

The first hot day of the year. BO *has a too-big rucksack on.* BETH *is working to control panic-attack breathing, eyes fixed on her feet.* BO *stops.* BETH *almost collides with her.* BO *drops the rucksack, stretches to the sky, does a bonkers little dance whilst also watching* BETH.

BO. THANK YOU SKY FOR MY THIRTEENTH-BIRTHDAY SKY. IT IS SUPERB. Thank you, thank you, thank you, Beth, above and beyond anything ever, this is even better than the sledge that Christmas when it snowed and we'd buggered all the baking trays and it's better than a dog, I know you'd never have got me a dog, I didn't want a dog, it's better than, it's better than, I don't know anything else I want. This is the best day. Thank you, Beth. I like that colour of sky an extreme amount.

BETH *has hands across her eyes.* BO *unpacks a rug (it's the shawl from the kitchen chair) and picnic stuff.*

I'm putting the rug out. There, you can sit here and sniff it. It still smells of kitchen. I just want this little picnic, then you can do some more pretending to be a driving instructor and I'll get us back quick-sticks, and no more attempting reverse before I can double declutch, promise, or speeding. I only went over sixty once and that was a straight bit so, you know, not bad, I can do it, we'll be back before you can say, slow the fuck down you maniac, even one more time.

BETH*'s breathing is steadying and gradually, over the next few minutes, returns to as close to regulated as* BETH *can manage out here under the great big sky.*

BETH. Migraine lifting. Finally.

BO. Jolly good.

BETH. Happy thirteen, my almost-grown, best beloved.

BO. Did you pack some water? Or no! I know, I bet I know! Is there home-made ginger beer?

BETH. Ha! D'you remember the year I made it for your birthday and the yeast and sugar did their thing, a little too vigorously, and it over-fermented and –

BETH *and* BO. Exploded.

BETH. Remarkable really, the synchronicity, six bottles, just like that. Pass the bag.

BO *does.* BETH *rummages, finds two bottles of Babycham, an opener and a jar of maraschino cherries.*

BO. Crikey O'Reilly, champagne!

BETH. But better. I had my first bottle of this at school, when I was a nipper.

BO. Come off it, no one would feed a four-year-old alcohol.

BETH. I hope you never have cause to know the horror people can inflict on babies and I didn't say four. This wasn't my first day! I was eight, or nine. D'you want to know the tale of my love affair with Babycham, or not?

BO. Sorry. Yes please.

BETH. Fingers on lips then. We had a house mother, she used to smuggle this in on birthdays, to cheer the miserable loneliness of imagining what it might be like to have a birthday surrounded by family. No doubt she was a raving alcoholic and any excuse, but it was meant kindly. There we'd sit, sucking away on our bottles of Babycham like it was milk, until she'd had enough of shushing our hysteria and she'd boot us out to weave our way back to the dorm. Birthday nights were the only time the sensation my heart was pounding in my head numbed. Silly really.

BETH*'s opened the cherries, poked one into each bottle.*
BETH *hands* BO *her bottle.*

There!

BO. What's the pink thing?

BETH. That, my darling, is a maraschino cherry. The only acceptable incarnation of that disappointing, borderline nasty, fruit.

BO. How will I get it out?

BETH. You won't. It will lend your first cocktail a mild marzipan flavour and then you will chuck it along with the bottle. Cheers. Here's to you, for all your days.

BO. And to you, for yours.

BETH. No! There's no need to share the toast, it's your birthday.

BO. But I want to.

BETH. You are a very good girl. Cheers.

BO. Cheers.

BETH *sips.* BO *downs her bottle.*

BETH. Way-up and slow down, soldier!

BO. It's only tiny. I was thirsty.

BO joggles the bottle trying to get the cherry out. BETH *passes the jar.* BO *takes one.*

How do you stop yourself eating the whole jar?

BETH. By doing it once. Alone. At night. Blurgh! There! Lucky you, again. You have me to test life's mistakes for you – so you don't have to.

BO. But can I try one more?

BETH. No. You're drunk. That's why you can't control your appetites.

BETH*'s rummaging, finds two oranges, a fruit knife and a box of sugar lumps.*

BO. Will I be too pissed to drive?

BETH. My guess is it'll improve things. Might slow you down. Catch. I can't believe I've never shown you this delicacy before.

She chucks an orange to BO.

What you have to do is squeeze and squash your orange, careful not to break the flesh, but keep going until you can feel it pulped to juice. It's most effective when you throw it lightly against a wall.

Mentioning a wall gives BETH *pause.* BO *notices. Keeps squashing. Quietness as they squash and watch the sea.*

BO. Has it made you think of being at home, saying about a wall? I'll be fine. It's been excellent.

BETH. The weather does seem to be turning, so possibly we should make a move, soonish.

The weather's unchanging.

BO. Do you wish you'd brought Keith with us?

BETH. I'm not sure I like Keith.

ACT ONE, SCENE NINE   51

BO. Really?! Brilliant. I don't like him at all. His teeth smell of cheese.

BETH *properly laughs. It relaxes her. A little.*

BETH. Oh my darling, that is so precisely it. How did you get close enough?

BO. You don't need to. He sort of wafts it into the room before him.

BETH. How could I have even contemplated kissing him, let alone have him to stay for, how long has it been?

BO. Five weeks three days, including today.

BETH. Okay. Let's ditch him on return.

BO. Yes! He's toast! Cheese on toast.

BETH. Drunkard. Is your orange soft?

BO. Feels like my new bosoms.

BETH *turns, looks at her child.*

BETH. Bo-Bo, I am so sorry. I didn't notice. How could I not have noticed my daughter has grown, what look like two perfect breasts? What is wrong with me?

BO. Nothing, please. I shouldn't have said, I feel stupid now, my periods haven't fully started or anything, it was just that one false start and sorry, about my, sorry. What do we do with the oranges?

BETH. Oh good god, please stop being so bloody nice. I didn't notice. I don't know when I stopped noticing. I don't think I did. I feel as if I stare at you all day long.

BETH *studies* BO.

BO. It's okay. I know I'm not beautiful. But I'm okay.

BETH. You're not a classical beauty, no. But I think you might just have some other thing, which is all your own. Thirteen is too young to tell. And you are a very young thirteen.

BO. Of course I am. I am one day on from being twelve.

BETH. Bit of birthday advice, as you teeter on the cusp of womanhood, try to sit on your pedantry. Men don't like clever women. Unless they are very, very clever and very, very beautiful. It's alright to be inadvertently funny but try and avoid /

BO. / Wit. I know. Honestly, I do know, you've said a gazillion times – slim is good thin is better, when you're in your dotage – little white pill or the pillow and nil, nil, nil by mouth! Men like... it's too boring, darling Mamma, but never Mamma, I'm always and only to call you Beth. You have a name. I know.

BETH. Good. So, when one's orange is soft as a firm breast, you cut a hole in the top... thus... then you insert a sugar lump into the hole... thus, then.

BETH *passes the orange. Prepares the other for herself.*

You suck the juice of the orange through the sugar.

BO. Are you cold?

BETH. Hm, starting to be.

BO *jumps up, tugs at the rug, offering it to* BETH.

BO. Here, wrap yourself up warm.

BETH *stands, pulls the shawl tight.*

BETH. You're going to be a beautiful mother, when your time comes.

BO. No ta! I don't want babies, there are enough babies in the world, I'm going to be a writer. Look! What is that bird? Its beak is like Effie Lump's trunk.

They watch the bird.

BETH. Which one?

BO. Silvery-grey but look, see its beak? Like the sharpest slither of moon. Crescent moon.

BETH. Or a nail clipping. Sorry. You're right. Its beak is like the moon. It's a curlew.

Music. BO *turns* BETH *and the split in the wall closes, cutting off our view of them.*

Film up.

A field beside a river. Day. Three small fruit-tree saplings, freshly planted. Bo's carrying a muddy spade, Ted's carrying Skylar. Skylar's wearing ear-defenders, pushing whilst clinging to Ted. They're grouped in a badly balanced triangle, looking at their trees.

BO. We can come once a year, see how much they've grown.

SKYLAR. Where's mine?

BO. We get to watch you grow every day. These three are just a private, private to us, way to remember. Your almost-sisters.

SKYLAR. It's not fair! I need trees!

BO. No, but it is right. You wouldn't be ours if I hadn't lost them.

SKYLAR. Oh my god you lost them?!

Scene Ten

On stage, BETH *runs into the kitchen, in the raggedy nightie she was in at the top of the play.* ***Film out.***

BETH. I'm coming!

BETH (*seventies*) *on stage alone. Sound of front door opening.* BO (*fifty*) *in.*

BO. Hello. It's me!

BETH *grabs a torch.* BO *isn't sure if* BETH *knows who she is.*

BETH. I need my husband.

BO. That's why I'm here. It's me, Bo, present and correct, fifty years your daughter. I'm here so Dominic can pop into work.

BETH. I do not heed you. I heed. No! Not that. Heed?

BO. Need.

BETH. What fucker needs what now?!

BO. I have a list of what medication you need to take when.

BETH. I am perfectly capable. I do this every day. All my fudge-fuck days!

BO. Of course you do. Are you, chilly?

BETH. I'm fucking ice to the blown! Bone?

BO. Here, let's wrap you up warm.

BETH. I can find my own raincoat, bloody fucking hell! My rain? Rainments!

BO wraps BETH in her shawl. BO's phone beeps, is silenced.

This is snuggly.

BETH tries to nestle BO.

What are these spikes called?

BO. Legs?

BETH. They're hot.

BO. They hurt?

BETH. They are fucking dying me.

BO's searching for meds, finds a tatty yellow notebook.

BO. Right, here's your list. Have you had your Aricept? Can I see if you made a note, please?

BO searches for meds.

BETH (*teary*). I know I've said this before but I think what you're doing with, with, her, La, that tiny, is the best thing you could be doing. You're saving a life.

BO. Yes, you have said.

BETH. I was a war baby, abandoned, did they tell you?

BO. But, do you think so, about saving her?

BETH. Yes, darling, I do. With every bit of me. All my titbits.

BO. Really, truly, I don't know.

BETH. Remember the air-raid siren? The patterns underneath the hall table? Their shelter. Skelter. Helter shelter. I wove a number of pieces based on those patterns. Do you know my work?

BO. Yup.

BETH. Are you a fan?

BO. I like the rug you made me. We still use it, actually.

BETH. Did I? Good. Ariadne's thread. To call oneself a true craftsperson one has to have made something for someone you love and have endured their indifference to it. I have endured.

BO. Yup. Me too.

BETH. That is absolute piffle. You have blot! Not like me! I can do that. I am perfectly capable. There's no need to dump me on the care system, just vet. Yet! That tiny doesn't like you.

BO. No, she really doesn't and, quite rightly, I don't think Ted does, any more.

BETH. She's just a child.

BO. She's not. Childlike.

BETH. She's not a bird! Terrible fucking name. Skylark?

BO. It's Skylar and, I didn't have the privilege of naming my child. Not that you've got a leg to stand on, when it comes to names.

BETH. Her, that tiny, is grief, she is grief-ing for her mother.

BO. I'm her mother!

BETH. Grief-ing for the one who pushed, hurt, that birth day one *and* you, her day by dahlia.

BO*'s sucker-punched by* BETH*'s crazy, perfect logic.*

Do you have a torch you might appendage me? Just until my husband lands.

Do you know him?

BO. That's why I'm here, so Dominic can go into work.

BETH. I need a torch, to fight my way!!

BO *hands* BETH *another torch.* BETH*'s breathing changes, she's managing a panic attack. She shines her big torch.*

Ex, ex, extra, big. And generally well-hung, that's the spill it. Ticket! Could you pass my medication notes?

BO *re-passes the yellow notepad.*

BO. Where are we up to?

BETH. We? What have you got?

BO. Nothing.

BETH. Lucky you. I am infested. But I am so lucky, my dearest, grand? Not the piano! The grand that goes on the journey with me?

BO. Skylar.

BETH. Her, that tiny, poor dear, she has so much more to grizzle than I. They were careless with her. No care. Not a care home?!

BO. I can't put you in a care home even if I wanted to, we don't have the paperwork. But you have to, truly you have to, let me get some help.

BETH. Dominic is right, you are a self-serving bitch! Out the fucking, out you go, slam the fudging, fucking off you fuck,

ACT ONE, SCENE TEN 57

how you leave, like no tomorrow, always leave, I am, I am more need!!

BO. Sorry if my good isn't good enough. I do have to be in London. For Skylar. And, actually, sorry, I want to be.

BETH. La, la, fucking La, you made your bed now you just have to lie about her.

BO. I am trying to.

BETH (*teary*). I know I've said this before but I think what you're doing with, with, her, La, that tiny is the best thing you could be doing. You're saving a life.

BO *presents meds.*

BO. Do you need some water, to swallow these with?

BETH. I was a war baby, abandoned, did they tell you?

BO. Take these pills then we can tick them off your list.

BETH. Abandoned!!

BO. Please will you swallow your pills?!

BETH. Fudges, fuck's sake, you, you who you are, when will you stop tidying me up?!

BETH *slaps* BO. BO, *practised at dodging Skylar's blows, ducks.* BETH *slaps again.* BO *grabs her wrist, holds it, tight. Stand-off.*

BO. What time is Dominic home?

BO*'s having another hot flush. Or is it anger? She releases* BETH.

BETH. Look at the colour in those cheeks! Tell you what, the fucking sweats are not joking. I'm still visited occupationally. You think your fudge is fucked! My fires almost overstated me. So put that in your fucking pie and choke on it!

BO. I know your menopause was a thousand times worse and I am sorry but please will you just take your meds, write

them in your book and stop comparing, just stop. Okay?
I know it's your fears, I know your fears...

BO's *phone beeps, she channels her exhaustion into texting. The word 'fear' unlocks* BETH. *She starts to sing the fourth verse of 'Both Sides Now' by Joni Mitchell.*

BO *puts down her phone. Watches* BETH, *who continues to sing.*

BO *lets her shoulders drop, joins the singing. They sing together until* BO *falters – the irony of the next lyric is too bald.* BETH *catches this change of mood, but half-sings on.*

BETH. I really don't know life at all.

A levelling beat. BO *picks up the torch, flicks it on, passes it.*

BO. Shall we brave the stairs?

BETH *shines the way. They leave the kitchen.*

BETH. I know I've said this before but I think what you're doing with, with, her, La, that tiny is the best thing you could be doing. You're saving a life.

Interval.

ACT TWO

Scene One

The sound of a large object being shunted into walls outside the kitchen. BETH (*early sixties*) *and* BO (*late thirties*) *offstage, grunting with effort.*

BO. It's too big.

BETH. We got it in therefore we can, and we will, get it out.

BO. *I* got it in and it was in pieces. We constructed it in your workshop.

BETH. Must you always appropriate every moment of my life? It can be your thirty-eighth-birthday prezzie, to yourself. Giving up appropriation. *I* got it in.

BO. Ow! That's my foot!

BETH. Sorry, darling. Shift it back a bit. Oof. It's fucking heavy.

BO. I'm the one holding all the weight!

BETH. Poor you. Oof!

One end of the huge object hits the wooden floor.

BO. Warn me! I'm still carrying my bit of the stupid bloody thing!

BETH. Every scrap of clothing you wore as a child, all meals devoured, the pony you wept and begged for, all of it, every bill, paid for from my toil at this loom.

BO. And how much did three weeks' worth of pony upkeep set you back? Is it safe for me to lower my end?

BETH. Why wouldn't it be?

BETH *enters the kitchen.*

BO. I can't see you, will I hurt you if I drop my end?

Silence from BETH.

Beth?!

BETH *starts packing pieces of her work into a box.*

Will I hurt you if I drop my end?

Silence.

Beth?!

BETH. Yes, darling?

BO. Unbelievable.

The other end of the loom's dropped, BO *negotiates past it.* BETH *continues to pack. Eventually,* BO *enters the kitchen. They don't make eye contact.*

Do you want to break for lunch?

BETH. What did you bring?

BO *to a bag, takes out Tupperware, cracks the lid, they peer inside.*

What is it?

BO. Veg curry.

BETH. And what, pray, are those luminous grey orbs?

BO. Eggs. Smells worse than the farts they'll cause.

BETH. What possessed you?

BO. It's very high in protein.

BETH. Shove it in the fridge. Dominic can fall upon it, on his return from the pub. If he ever does return.

BO. Shall we have a coffee?

BETH. I suppose we'll have to.

BO *makes two black coffees,* BETH *continues to pack.*

BETH. Thank you for giving up your precious working day to help me.

BO. What time are you due at the craft fair?

BETH. Exhibition!

BETH *brandishes a small woven wall-hanging.*

What do you think these are, crochet doilies?!

BO. You remain confident we'll get your loom unstuck, delivered to this village hall and, if we do, there'll be enough room to set up your demonstration, alongside the WI cakes and that inevitable nutter who paints baby animals on pebbles – yes?

BETH *stops folding. She lays a piece on the table.*

BETH. This is called – 'A Longed-For Dawn' – I spent a week at the coast planning it, I was there from four in the morning – gazing at where I guessed the horizon lay, searching the colours for their essence. I mixed the dyes myself. Fifteen attempts to weave before I was satisfied. I'm sorry I can't seem to get myself further than some poky little community centre to show my pieces but that doesn't mean it isn't my work.

BO *gives* BETH *coffee, picks up the sculpture, studies it.*

BO. How did you get yourself to the sea?

BETH. I have been defending your rudeness to Dominic for years, did you know? He says you're self-serving.

BO. I'll bet he does.

BETH. What's that supposed to mean?

BO. There's no way you drove yourself to the sea, is there? Do *you* know he phones me, leaves messages on the answerphone demanding respite? He hangs up if I answer.

BETH. Respite?! I am sixty-two! I am at the peak of my creative powers. Fucking hell, I am more attractive, my skin is tight, my hair is, well it's only a tad silver, but fuck, I'm a goddess compared with any woman he might ever... Bloody, bloody hell, respite?

BO. Sorry. Hey, he's right, I am a selfish cow.

BETH *gets up, finds an ancient biscuit tin, proffers its contents.*

Oh my god, chocolate idiot biscuits. You haven't made these for years.

She takes a biscuit, drinks her coffee.

BETH. I have. I make them in secret. For myself alone. Dominic has never even sniffed a chocolate idiot, let alone tasted one.

BO. Good.

BETH. Yes. Fuck him.

BO. I don't want to think about that.

BETH. Me neither. Not in these trousers! Bleugh! How's Ted?

Silence.

I know! You've told me, many painful times, your life-transforming therapist has instructed you not to speak to me about your sex life.

BO. I ditched her.

BETH. Right. Gosh. Why? When?

BO. About a month ago.

BETH. I am aware I should say something neutral and supportive but I simply can't. I am too, too thrilled.

BO. Thought you might be.

BETH. So? Tell. Why?

BO. I was cleverer than her. I kept making her cry. It made me want to punch her.

BETH. Oh please, I beg, tell me you did?

ACT TWO, SCENE ONE 63

BO (*imitating ex-therapist*). I'm noticing you're carrying a lot of unexpressed rage, Bethan. Would you like to say more about that?

BETH (*gleeful*). No, no – it's my daughter, she's the vicious one.

BO. Mmm-hmm. I wonder what would happen if you gave yourself permission to feel whatever it is her viciousness is bringing up for you.

BETH. Punch myself?

BO. I started making stuff up. Challenged myself to knock a minute off each week before she cried. On the day I fired her, I had to hand her the tissues. Eighteen minutes.

BETH. When I had my therapy it took three weeks before I convinced him of the necessity to offer his services gratis, and four before he asked if I understood the nature of transference at which juncture, naturally, he got his cock out. I remember it vividly. Looked shockingly like a parsnip. Unnervingly tapered end.

BO. It wasn't my therapist who told me to tell you to stop going on and on about sex. I made that up too.

BETH. So you are clever, but not clever enough to fire her before you'd shelled out Christ-knows-how-much lolly merely to indulge your thwarted writer's instincts.

They eat biscuits. BETH *returns to packing.* BO *shakes crumbs from the piece on her lap.*

BO. How much will you charge for this?

BETH. A total pittance. Forty quid. If I can get it. I'll do what I usually do, chat them up, work out the maximum I think they can afford and come in a tenner cheaper.

BO. How much would you charge me?

BETH. Full forty. A fool and their money and all that.

BO *gets out a chequebook, writes a cheque, hands it over.*

That's a lot of money. What's it for?

BO. For 'A Longed-For Dawn'. What it's worth. To me.

BETH *stares at the miraculous cheque.*

It's worth more but that's the absolute max I can afford.

BETH. It is worth more.

BO. Even if you were only assessing its worth on an hourly rate.

BETH. Not to mention whatever a person charges for materials, experience, craft.

BO. Art.

BETH. Yes. Art.

BETH *pops the cheque in a pocket.* BO *joins in packing.*

I'd never charge you, under normal circs, but just at the mo I'm the tiniest bit short.

BO. You can think of it as commission.

BETH. Don't patronise me, darling. I am not your ex-therapist. You've paid the correct price for a piece of work you adore. That's all.

It's hard for BO *to tell* BETH *what she wants to.*

BO. Remember I told you about that telly idea I pitched?

BETH. Which one? I've lost count.

BO. This one's been commissioned. Properly. I've signed a contract. There're dates to start filming.

BETH. Oh darling, darling Bo-Bo, at last!

BO. It's loosely based on that lumpy blob you wove for me, when I was a kid. Remember, Effie the Lump?

BETH. Are you telling me I did something right?! That something I made for you as a child has turned to gold?!

BO. Yes. Um. Thank you.

BETH. It's my unmitigated pleasure!

BO. I thought you'd be disappointed it was for children and not a grown-up drama, be disappointed in me.

BETH. You are the strangest most mysterious girl I've ever had the joy to encounter. I am bursting with pride!

BO. In yourself?

BETH. I'm happy.

BETH's smile slides away, until her face is blank.

BO. Very funny.

BETH slips sideways.

There's no need to take the piss.

BO gives BETH a little push. Nothing.

Beth?

Nothing.

Woo-hoo?

Nothing.

Please stop it.

Nothing.

Are you okay?

BETH opens glazed eyes. Mumbles.

BETH. My head is full of clouds.

Film up.

An X-ray of a brain.

Black on indigo. Sound of hospital, beep of life support, beep of text on Bo's phone, 'When You Smile' – far away, underwater. BO *and* BETH *turn to watch the film, stare at the brain.* ***It looks like the moon seen from the field.***

On stage, BETH *shakes her muddled head, stumbles to bed.*

The brain's 'clouds' speed up, race. BO *exits kitchen, and hospital.*

Film out.

Scene Two

On stage, BETH in bed, alone. Groans. Twitching. Struggling with blanket. Gets her hand under, starts rubbing. It looks masturbatory.

CAROL enters with yogurt, doesn't notice rubbing, lifts BETH to feed her. She removes the apparently masturbatory hand.

CAROL. Upsadaisy, Mrs Lazy. Here we go.

Here we go. Open up. Good and wide. Cherry. No bits. Open up for what we are about to receive.

CAROL tries to prise open BETH's mouth. BETH bites.

Ow! That is not nice. You are not that kind of person. Be nice. Open up. Now. Have a little taste, you do need to, ever such a lot. It's not right to be so hungry. We can't have you going around nibbling people, can we?

BETH. Cock off.

CAROL out, calling down the corridor.

CAROL. Has anyone seen the duty doctor?! It's Beth, she spoke! Bless her. She's sat right up eating lunch and she spoke. Who's on duty?!

BETH's hand returns, slowly, under the covers. Rubbing. Groaning. Tears. BO enters.

BO. Hello.

*BO spots the mess in BETH's mouth, gets water and a cotton bud. **Film on.***

Bo's bathroom. Day.

Bo has her head over the bath, demonstrating, using a handheld shower. Skylar's pinned to the wall, clutching shampoo.

It's easy-peas. You do Mummy then I'll /

Skylar chucks the shampoo at Bo.

SKYLAR. / You're not my mum!!

> BETH *opens her mouth, lets* BO *clean her. **The shampoo hits Bo.***
>
> ***Film out.***

BO. It's only thrush, looks a bit claggy but it's okay. I'm getting rid of that. There. It doesn't hurt, does it?

> BO *washes.* BETH *restarts her agonising journey to rubbing.*

Jesus, Beth, stop it! Not now. You can't do that in a hospital! Not like that.

> BETH *scrabbles.* BO *calls.*

Excuse me?! So sorry but please could you help me, for a second?! My mother?!

> PAULINA *enters.*

Thank you, very much.

PAULINA. Hello, Bo, isn't it? I haven't seen you for a while, how do you find Bethan?

BO. Beth. Yes, so sorry not to be able to get here more often, it's just my mother, she, I feel a bit odd saying this but she appears to be, she did always enjoy, it looks so...

PAULINA. Yes. Bethan? That looks unpleasant. Her husband /

BO. / Dominic.

PAULINA. Her husband says she's suffered from this for /

BO. / Suffered? Did he actually say that?

PAULINA. I'm going to find someone to administer some pain /

BO. / Is she in pain? Why would it be hurting her? Do other people, have you seen this, touching like this, before?

PAULINA. It's quite normal for people to /

BO. / Yes, obviously, normally, but at this stage, do people?

PAULINA. Please don't worry, it'll be /

BO. / Is she in pain?!

> PAULINA *exits. BO's still misreading* BETH's *movements as sexual, and this as a potential climax.* BETH's *crying with pain, scratching to relieve intense irritation caused by thrush.* BO *lifts the covers, tries to take* BETH's *hands.*

> Oh my Christ you have to stop, please, you've got to stop! You're bleeding quite badly there's bits of flesh oh you poor...

> BO *to the door.* BETH's *attempting to scratch.*

> Stop it! You've got to stop it, now!

> BO *exits to get help, in the corridor, collides with* CAROL.

> (*Off.*) Sorry. Let me help pick those up, please I need help!

CAROL. Have you been in with her? Isn't it lovely?

BO. No. She's covered /

They re-enter.

CAROL. / What's going on here? This won't do. What have you /

BO. / Nothing, nothing at all. She's raw, there's so much blood, down there. It's not me.

CAROL. Nothing indeed. Beth, you hold on, just one minute, the doctor's asked me to give you something for your sciatica. I've got it right here.

BO. What?! What sciatica? Who said?

CAROL. Your dad. Very concerned he's been and now look at her and she was so bright at lunch.

BO. He's not my father, what lunch?

> CAROL's *preparing a syringe.*

Stop. It's got nothing to do with her leg. It's not that. Look. Look at her vagina. Beth, please stop, please!

CAROL *lifts the blanket. Both arrested by* BETH*'s bloodied thighs and vagina.* BETH*'s whimpering, weeping.*

How long has she been scratching at herself like this?

CAROL. I don't know. I've not seen her at it.

BO. How do you know about Dominic saying it's sciatica?

CAROL. He said. Her legs. Her twitching. Aching. I suppose a bit of rubbing.

BO. Like this? Rubbing like this? For how long?

CAROL. Since she came in.

BO. Why hasn't anyone checked? Who washes her? How could you think it's sciatica?

CAROL. There's no need, he said, your dad said. I'm not a doctor.

BO. What can you give her? You need to stop it hurting her. Now. She's in too much pain. Please.

CAROL. Emollient. That's what she needs.

BO. You are fucking joking. Please do not tell me this is just thrush.

CAROL. I will not take abuse from you.

BO. Great. Don't. Get me a doctor and some serious painkiller. Now.

CAROL *exits.* BO *searches the room, her handbag.* BETH*'s scratching, whimpering.*

Leave yourself alone. Please! Let it alone! Look, look what I've found!

BO *proffers Sudocrem.* BO *holds* BETH*'s hands, pot between her teeth, scoops a dollop.* BO *braces, wipes* BETH*'s thighs and vagina.* BETH*'s whimpering turns to sexual-sounding relief.* BO *finishes.*

I'm giving you some cream because you have some kind of infection. That's why I'm touching you. I think you've got yourself infected.

BETH *moans, little yelps where cream's sinking into raw flesh. Animal, sex sounds.*

This is, it's barrier cream, to stop you hurting.

PAULINA, CAROL *and* JILL *enter.*

I was, I gave her some emollient, I was so worried she's, doing that, touching herself, that seems to have got her infected, I did what you said, see, Sudocrem.

PAULINA. Hi, right-o, this seems to have got a little out of /

BO. / There was no one to help, she was in such pain, look at her, I gave her some Sudocrem.

PAULINA. Carol, have you got that pain relief?

CAROL *moves to administer the shot.*

BO. Stop a minute. What's that?

PAULINA. We are moving to the next level of pain relief. Nothing we do here is going to prolong life and I am not implying that you want /

BO. / Yes, but for what?

PAULINA. Precise diagnosis may not /

CAROL. / She spoke.

BO. Please do not say things like that.

JILL. Carol love.

PAULINA. Would you like a cup of coffee? Jill, could you?

BO. Why did she have lunch? What did she have?

PAULINA. Now is the time to move to the next level. I'm sorry but we need to reattach the drip. This can also help with anxiety, at a later date. To ease her. We understand /

CAROL. / Excuse me but she did speak.

BETH *moans*.

JILL. She has had quite bad thrush.

JILL *points out notes about emollient and thrush to* PAULINA.

BO. In her mouth, this is, isn't this caused by, her, pleasure? Comfort?

PAULINA. Thank you, Jill. She may also have had pains commonly diagnosed as sciatica but this, categorically, those lesions, are caused by Bethan scratching herself to relieve the discomfort caused by thrush. This is thrush. It's a nasty infection, which can have sprung to this level overnight as the surface of her skin is, naturally, frail. What we need to do now is administer the appropriate pain relief. Carol? Jill?

CAROL. Can I suggest you wash your hands?

JILL. Let's get you that coffee and, Carol, can get on with things here. You can wash next door.

JILL *leads* BO *off, who calls*.

BO. What did she have for lunch?!

Film up.

Beach. Day.

Edge of the sea, looking up a beach towards the shore. On the horizon Bo, Skylar and Beth running towards the sea, arms helicopter-twirling. Arriving at the swash, they leap in the air.

A loud knocking at the front door outside the kitchen. CAROL *exits*.

Film freezes with Bo, Skylar and Beth mid-jump.

Film out.

Scene Three

BETH, *on stage, sits painfully up.*

BETH. Fudge off, fuck off you, off, special off, fuck-offer.

Another knock. BETH (*seventies*) *drags her failing body into the kitchen.*

Hello?

BETH *grabs an industrial-sized torch.*

Door being kicked.

Mercy! Pray you! Mercy me!

BO (*fifty-one*) *enters.* BO's *carrying bags of ready meals.* BETH *studies her. Lowers her torch.*

BO. We have to get that door seen to.

BETH. Dominic can give it a bloody good, suing? Seeing! Seeing, as you asked.

BO. That'll be a first.

BETH. Yes, I'll buggy say. Did he give up on you too?

BO. Not sure he even knows my name.

BETH. What is your fuckwit?

BO. Bo, present and correct, fifty-one years your daughter.

BETH. Poor you. I have so little medication. All of it efficacious.

Shows BO *her yellow notebook.*

In here.

BO. Let me see.

BETH *guards her book.*

Fine, where's your blister pack? I need to check where you're up to.

BETH. Please do not sully me. I know you're ready to bumhole me off into some care home, homeless, home on the range, range, rage! Argh! Don't hit me!!

BO. Stop it! No one is going to hit you. I just need to make sure you've taken the pills you're supposed to have taken. Give.

BETH. Ner, ner, ner ner ner.

BO. Please, please give me the sodding book or pack or Dominic's list or whatever. Now.

Stand-off.

BETH. You do not scare me. You bitch! Not one snot. One fudging, fucking jittery jot!

During this next, unseen by BO, BETH slips sideways.

BO. You're right. What difference does it make if you take it or not? News flash. There's no point to your medication. I have been driving since five a.m. It has taken me four and a half hours to get here. I am here for one hour. I am then going to meet a nice-ish woman who is going to come in every day, who knows, she might even wash your hair and I know you can do it but she will do it better. She will do it. I have –

Her phone rings.

Oh for god's sake, now what?! (*Answers her phone.*) ...School of course, they want her picking up immediately... She climbed on top of the cupboard... chucking stuff, something hit the PTA woman's Little Princess On Board... You know where I am, with my fucking mother!... Can you stop being nice about Dominic!... Because it's traditional for stepchildren to hate the usurping adult.

Ted's hung up.

Film up.

Bo's bedroom. Night.

Bo awake in bed beside a sleeping Ted. Skylar calls, terrified, from her room.

SKYLAR. Come, come, come!

Bo shoots upright.

Film out.

On stage, BO *turns to* BETH.

BO. Beth? Hello?

Nothing.

Stop it. Okay, let's find that blister pack. What do we need next? Okay fine, I'll cancel the hair washer.

BO *backs off. Nudges* BETH. *Nothing.* BO *retreats, eyes on* BETH. *Dials 999.*

Hello. Ambulance please… My mother… She's had a… She has a memory-related thing but this is… I think she's had another stroke… Please.

Film up.

Bo, Skylar and Beth still frozen in mid-air. Film we've seen of them running towards the swash rewinds. Runs speeded up and backwards – their arms helicopter-twirling, they look like a pastiche of people swimming backstroke.

Onstage, three PARAMEDICS *enter the kitchen.*

PARAMEDIC ONE. Bethan? Is it? Hello, Bethan?

PARAMEDIC TWO. How long do you say she's been like this?

PARAMEDIC THREE. What've you been up to, young lady?

BO. It's Beth.

PARAMEDIC ONE. Beth? We're here to help.

Film out. *Sound of the sea swells.*

PARAMEDIC THREE. Is there an advance directive?

PARAMEDIC ONE. On my count.

BO. No. But.

PARAMEDIC TWO. Overnight bag?

PARAMEDIC ONE. One, two, three, lift.

PARAMEDICS *lift* BETH.

Film up.

A body dives underwater – in a swimming pool.

BO. I'm so sorry, she's a bit smelly. Sorry. I have been trying. I'll get some of her stuff.

BO *exits*. PARAMEDICS *carry* BETH *to bed. The drip's reattached.*

On film, there's an exploded trail of bubbles left by the diving body. Leaving a watery glow, which grows into the surface of a swimming pool. Film plays on.

PARAMEDICS *pack equipment, exit.*

Scene Four

The back wall splits, creating an aperture, to the side of BETH*'s bed,* BO *(five) is revealed, apparently sitting on the edge of the* **swimming pool.** BO *and* BETH *play this scene, from their respective positions on stage.* **We see and hear the Lengths Swimmer on film.**

BO. Mum-mum-mum-meeeeee?! Watch! Watch! I am going to do an enormous diving. Mummy?! Watch meeeeee!

LENGTHS SWIMMER (*on her way past, on film, speaking to* BO, *live, on stage*). **How old are you?**

BO. I'm pretty close to being six.

LENGTHS SWIMMER. You with someone?

BO. My mummy's doing floating.

LENGTHS SWIMMER. Don't come too close.

BO. I am probably entering exams for doing a specially long bit of swimming any day now.

LENGTHS SWIMMER. Right-o. Can you swim?

BO. Generally. I can do the breathing.

LENGTHS SWIMMER. Want me to catch you?

BO. Nah. I'm doing testing out, for coldness.

LENGTHS SWIMMER. It's fine once you're in. Enjoy your specially long swim.

Lengths Swimmer dives down, and off. The surface of the swimming pool remains on film.

BETH (*twenties, as if she's swum over*). What did that nosy cow want?

BO. For me to dive right in.

BETH. Jesus Christ what a maniac. You can't swim. Did you tell her you can't swim?

BO. Course. She said she'd do catching.

BETH. I am in charge of catching. Got that? The world is riddled with absolute maniacs. Never ever let any of them near you and especially not your body. It's yours for you alone. Understood?

BO. What about please and thank you to maniacs on buses?

BETH. Don't twist things, you know what I mean. I'm talking about actual maniacs.

BO. Is she an actual maniac?

BETH. Certified.

On film, the Lengths Swimmer's looking back, checking on Bo. BO *flicks a V.*

What the hell was that for?

BO. For her certified.

BETH. Ha, ha, ha. Very good.

BETH *flicks too.* ***The Lengths Swimmer's puzzled then flicks in return.***

Yes, yes, fuck right off, lady. Byeee.

Lengths Swimmer exits. Swimming-pool film plays on.

Right, let's swim. Jump. No. Run, from as far back as you can, let rip an ear-busting scream, then jump higher than an electrocuted flea and I will catch you! Go!

BO. I want to use those steps.

BETH. Don't be such a baby. Jump. It's the only way.

BO*'s waving her legs in the water.*

BO. Coldish.

BETH. Bloody freezing. Come on! Jump!

BETH *splashes* BO. BO *splashes back.* BO *loses her balance, slides into the water.*

BO. Weeeeeeee!

BETH. Well done, Little Flea. You're in! You can swim.

BO. I did a lot of drinking.

BETH. Try to keep your mouth closed next time. People pee in swimming pools. Swimming pools have a Pavlovian effect on the bladder. Out you get. Good. Now jump, again.

BO. I am a little bit full up of all that pee now.

BETH. Piffle. Have a good spit and in we go.

BO. Will I go diving again?

BETH. You will and I will catch you. Stop dithering. Don't think about it. Jump.

BO. I can't stop the thinking.

BETH. Ha. No. Well, keep on thinking but whilst you're solving the mysteries of life, get on with it. I'm catching pneumonia hanging around in here. Jump!

BO. I'm catching the new moaner too.

BETH. Whose fault it that? Buggering hell, Bo, come on.

BETH *waves to an unseen onlooker.*

BO. Is François watching?

BETH. But of course. Can't take his bulgy blue eyes off me.

BO. And me.

BETH. Come on! Full flea, please!

BO. I need a pee.

BETH. Jump. I'll catch you, float you to the side, then you can do it.

BO. In the pool?

BETH. But absolutely nowhere near me. Wait till I've got out.

BO. Who will hold me from drowning?

BETH. No one. You will hold yourself. Jump.

BO. Catch me?

BETH. Course.

BO. Weeeeeeeeee!

Bo leaps into the pool, surfaces, Beth catches her. We see this on film.

BETH. Good. Hold it in until I'm out! Oh yuck! Stop it! That is revolting. You filthy child.

BO. That is toasty.

BETH. Ha, ha, ha. Ecstasy, isn't it? But only if it's your own. You are never to do that near me again, understood? Or I swear I will drown you.

BO. Like you did the kittens?

BETH. Exactly like the kittens. Hold still, I'm going to flip you round onto your back and you are going to float, like I was doing whilst you were flirting with the maniac.

ACT TWO, SCENE FOUR   79

BETH *flips* BO.

BO. Argh. No, I said no to the flip.

BETH. You're fine. Let go. I'm taking your head. Just let go. Let your body float. You'll still be here but it'll feel like flying in a dream.

BO. I can't.

Beth takes Bo's head. We see this on film.

BETH. Oh but you can. See? Breathe out in a long puff.

BO *does*.

Pretend your head's a sack of sand getting wetter and wetter. How does sand feel when it's wet?

BO. Thick.

BETH. Heavy. And thick. Like the maniac. Heavier head, give your head to me. That's it. There we go.

On film, Beth's swooshing Bo from side to side, cradling her head.

Grey goose and gander, waft your wings together and carry the good king's daughter over the one-strand river.

Wotcha.

BO. Keep me held.

BETH. I'm not letting go. I'm swapping your head for holding a hand. It's fine. I've still got you and now we're together.

Both splayed, holding one hand.

Puff out your breath. Excellent breathing. Now, join in. Grey goose and –

BETH *and* BO. – gander, waft your wings together and carry the good king's daughter over the one-strand river.

They float on.

You are a water baby.

One more jump. Out you get. Good. Ready?

They're out.

BO. Not quite.

> BETH *and* BO *take hands. They jump.* **On film, we see Bo and Beth leaping into the pool.**

BETH. Flyyyyyiiiiiiinnnnnnggggggg.

> ***They're in.*** *Music. The aperture closes on* BO *onstage.* BETH *lays back.*

> **On film: Bo and Beth, underwater. Umbilical, timeless memory. Slow motion, travelling, twisting, dancing underwater. Separate, together. Until the film fades, leaving a watery glow.**

> *Music still playing. Night in the hospital.* BETH*'s alone, pained breathing echoes unnaturally, with the music.*

> **On film: this next floats on top of the watery glow.**

> **Skylar's bedroom. Night.**

> **Volume of the music dips. Skylar asleep under the rug and table. Bo awake lying on the floor. Skylar jolts awake, terrified, oblivious to Bo.**

SKYLAR. Come, come, come!!

> ***Bo reaches out a hand, places it, gently, onto Skylar's head.***

BO. I am come.

> *Music out.* ***Film fades.***

Scene Five

BO *enters the hospital. Sits beside the bed. It's now day.*
BETH*'s exactly as was.* BO*'s watching* BETH *intensely.*
JILL *appears.*

JILL. Cup of tea? Coffee? They do a nice cheese sarnie in the canteen?

BO. No. But thank you, you're kind.

JILL. You'd be welcome. You sure?

BO. I'm fine. Thanks.

> JILL *goes.* BO *returns to watching.* JILL *passes back.* BO *to the door, eyes on* BETH.
>
> Jill? Could I? Very quickly? Sorry.

JILL. Yes, my lovely, shall I get you that coffee? Even just some water?

BO. No, really, thank you. I'm so sorry to ask, I know you can't know but if it's possible to plan, which I know it isn't but...

JILL. I've seen people asking for a relative in Australia, hanging on three weeks, ten minutes after that person arrives, it's over. Or, there was a lovely lady sat with her dad, must have been over forty hours, wouldn't even use the toilet, so sad, she had to in the end, second she was out the room her mum just went. They choose.

BO. I don't want to miss it.

JILL. I don't think you will, if she wants you here. We'll call you the second there's any change.

> JILL *makes to leave.*

BO. Has she spoken to, anyone, Carol, or anyone?

JILL. No, she hasn't, not for a while now.

> JILL *watches* BO *watching* BETH.
>
> There's another thing. Happened with my mum but I've seen it I don't know how many times now.

BO. What?

JILL. At the end, it's like the dementia, or whatever, it's like it's not there, not in the same way, like the bit of them that's, them, that bit comes back, in some way.

JILL leaves.

A different day. BETH's *unchanged.* BO's *in the chair. Eventually* BO *reaches and strokes* BETH's *hair. She keeps her hand on* BETH's *head.*

BO, *quietly, slowly sings 'When You Smile' by Shirley Bassey.*

BETH *turns, and opens her eyes. She joins in. Her voice is almost only air.*

Film pulses, faintly to life.

Bo's kitchen. Day.

Bo (late forties), Beth (late sixties) at the table. Bo's leaking tears, shattered by tiredness. Beth holding a coffee.

BETH. What you're doing with Skylar is the best thing you could be doing. You're saving a life.

On film, Beth places the coffee down. *On stage,* BO *stands. **Film out.***

Scene Six

BETH *raises herself. A moment of acknowledgment. Into the kitchen. It's night.* BETH *walks through.* BO *takes meringues out of the bottom oven. Stirs food. Calls.*

BO. All fine. So, I'm moving this onto the slow plate?

BETH (*off*). For heaven's sake, darling, you're twenty-two, do you really need baby steps for everything? Work it out. Is the pan burnt dry? No. Are its contents cremated? No. Does it taste okay? Yes. Ta-dah. Supper.

Bubbles please.

BO *exits plus bottle. Music upstairs.* BETH *enters. More beautiful than should be possible. To the stove. Tastes. Calls.*

Darling?

BO. Yeah.

BETH. I hate to criticise but did you taste this?

BO. Um. I think so.

BETH. Don't fib. I refuse to believe you have so little of me in you. You couldn't possibly have tasted this. Bring the wine. Lickety-spit.

BO *enters, plus wine.*

Big shloosh in there then get some herbs. This is shockingly bland.

BO *does as she's told.*

And, darling, but really, it's New Year's sodding Eve, do you think it might be possible to greet the year with just the teeniest bit of oomph? Some feeble attempt at loveliness? A Greenham Common woolly? You have a sweet body but really, darling.

BO*'s out the back door.*

BO. I know, I know. I wanted to be comfy.

BETH. It's hotter than a furnace in here.

BETH's *having a hot flush, she laps up the icy blast.*

BO (*calling*). Rosemary, thyme or sage?

BETH. Sage?! Are you mad? Rosemary.

BO *back, both to the stove. Companionable cooking.*

Rosemary for remembrance. Smell – (*Proffers bunch.*) bog-cleaner, no?

BO. Um, there's something I think you should know. I wondered about asking your advice.

BETH. How thrilling. Are you in love? No, let me guess. You've written a novel! No? Love. Must be love. Who is he?! It's not that boy who made a pass at me?! The one that walks like a policeman?

BO. Ted?! He offered to buy you a drink because he was walking past and didn't want you to feel odd about hanging around the student bar because he's, he's kind, but not in a soppy way, in the way of a person who has thought about kindness and decided it's for them. And he doesn't walk like anything, he walks like Ted.

BETH *twinkles.*

It is possible to just be friends with a boy, you know!

BETH. Who then? Do they adore that horrid lesbian woolly, is that why you're insisting on it? Come on, tell Mumma.

BO. I had a one-night stand.

BETH. Finally, finally! And? More than one, I trust?

BO. No, sorry, just the one. I went to the maddest dinner party. Some girl I'd never even spoken to at university. No idea why she invited me. It was so posh. Hundreds of small dogs and a candelabra. I got /

BETH. / Pissed?

BO. Yes. Very.

BETH. So? And? The sex? Nice cock?

BO. I don't know. My bra had holes in it. He tried to sneak off at five in the morning but I woke up. I told him I wanted him to sneak off. Made him do a stupid quiz because he couldn't remember my name.

BETH. None of this is the point of a one-night stand. The point is untrammelled uninhibited selfishness.

BO. Not a baby then?

BETH. Well yes, in your case.

BO. Really?! I was a one-night stand?! Really?!

BETH. Yes. A glorious one and we did hook up together after, as you know, but essentially, yes. I truly fucked you into being. I knew exactly what I was up to. Made sure I came and came and came. You were created on the ocean of love.

BO. How could it be love?

BETH. Real love not sickly pointless headfuck ideas-based control-freak love. Love from and for the body. My body. The body as an engine built to create.

BO. I'm pregnant.

BETH. For keeps?

BO. I need an abortion. Pretty sharpish. I've been a bit of a twonk. Dithered. I'm very pregnant.

BETH. Well thank the gormless goddess for that, explains the maternity wear. I forgive you the sack. Now, when I had my abortion it was in Bristol and, strangely, it was simply hugely comforting. Myself, back, for myself again. I'll never forget the smell of the anaesthetic as I came round, burying my face in the pillow to fill my lungs, sucking it in so it would never leave me. I can smell it now, if I try. (*Sniffs hard.*) Mmmm. That smell will live inside me for ever. Until I succumb to the old dementch, which no doubt I will and whilst we're on the subject, darling, when I do succumb, you're not to forget – little white pill or the pillow, which ever comes to hand and, absolutely, nil by mouth, and, never ever abandon me in one of those supposed care places. Promise?

BO. Yup, I know, I know, promise. You won't get anything like that. You remember everything. Where in Bristol?

BETH. I do and I will. Promise? Nil by mouth?

BO. I've said a gazillion times. Where in Bristol and how much was it?

BETH. Gawd knows. I'll have written it down somewhere. Do you have money?

BO. Not a bean. Can I?

BETH. Don't ask me. Let's call your one-night stand. Least he could do, unmemorably cocked fucker, trying to sneak out on us. Let's call him.

BO. I don't know his name. I told him I didn't want his number and I don't. Turning up pregnant is just so badly organised, and I didn't know how to make him come and I /

BETH. / Enough said. I will lend you the money. You will have to pay it back as I am on my utter uppers until Dominic the Dreary moves in, and I charm my first rent cheque, but that's only next week. Sure you don't want to have her?

BO. I'm not like you. I don't seem to have maternal instincts.

BETH. Not to worry. Plenty of time. You, have to do something first. Be something. Then you can prematurely age me into grannyhood, only please remember your tinies are never ever to call me fucking granny. It was bad enough enduring your 'mummy' phase.

BO. Yes, Beth. Thank you, Beth.

BETH. You are welcome, Boudicca. Daughter.

They smile wryly.

I am sorry for your germ. Such a waste. But there we go.
Down the hatch and let's dance. Go and put on something
jolly.

BO *knocks back her drink, goes upstairs.* BETH *to back
door. Directs hot flush into the night – overwhelming rage –
wipes sweat off her face. Silent hot tears. Music from
upstairs.* BETH *finds a yellow notepad, writes.* BO *in.*
BETH *notices* BO's *changed her clothes.*

Blessings on you for all your days, always make an effort,
darling. I'm sorry to say but you do need to. Some people
don't, and lucky them, but we do. Make sure you always do.
Buck up and all will be well.

BETH *holds out a hand. Lazy much-practised ironic jive.*

This nest will be yours one day. It is yours now, only I do
need to squat in it. Temporarily.

JILL *and* CAROL *enter the hospital. Watch the dancing.*
JILL *holds a hand to* BETH *who dances to the bed.* BO
watches the film.

Film up.

Car. Day. Country lane.

Bo in the car, phone on her lap on speaker.

**CALLER. I'm calling from the hospital. Your dad said we
should call. Your mum's breathing has changed.**

BO. Is this it?

CALLER. Where are you?

**BO. I'm nearly there. Please, will you tell her I'm coming?!
And, please, please can you tell her, I will keep trying.**

In the hospital, CAROL *leaves,* JILL's *watching* BETH.
BETH's *breathing's worse.*

BO *steps into the hospital.* JILL *leaves.*

Scene Seven

Film out. *BO helps a weak and weary* BETH *upright.* BETH *(thirties) and* BO *(ten) crouched on* BETH*'s bed, as if in the doorway of a shop.* BETH*'s attempting to control a panic attack.*

BETH. I'm going to fall.

BO. You're not. I can get Leonard, he said he'll be in the record shop. He said only ten minutes. He did say wait near the phone box, Mummy.

BETH. Beth! I am a person. I have a name. You are ten years old, please act your age.

BO. Yes, sorry, Beth.

BO makes to go.

BETH. No! Stop! Don't leave me! I can't get a breath in. You have to help me!

BO. It is okay, you can breathe. Big breath. I can call the operator for the record shop. (*Rummages in* BETH*'s handbag.*) We need a two p. Or a ten p.

BETH. Not fucking ten, two!

BO. There's no money.

BETH*'s panic-breathing intensifies.*

Please, Beth, breathe.

BETH *tries, clinging to* BO. *Sinking.*

You can not fall. Get up! Stop it.

BETH. Do not tell me how to be. I can't! I am falling. I can feel air passing through my heart. Oh, Leonard?! Help me!

BO. Leonard isn't here.

BETH. Argh no! Has he left? Where is he? I need him!

BO. I can help you. You said, you said Leonard mustn't see one of these panic attacks. Come on. Stand up.

BETH. What did I do wrong? Oh, falling!

ACT TWO, SCENE SEVEN   89

BO. Shush. Shush. Please. There are people.

BETH. I know about the fucking people! People are the fucking problem. Get me home! I need to get home!

BETH starts to shiver.

BO. Beth?

BETH. I'm extraordinarily cold.

BO. Where?

BETH. Everywhere. I'm too cold. Pneumonia. My lungs are filling with water. Argh. My leg. I've seized. I'm falling.

BO. Please don't be too cold. Please don't fall. I'm going to hot potato you.

BO does.

BETH. There's a hole inside me.

BO. Please, oh please, let me help you.

BETH. No. Ask someone, say, my mother's man has disappeared and we need one urgently. He's called, oh, how silly, what's he called?

JILL and CAROL enter.

BO. We don't need their help. I'm here.

BETH. I need all the help I can get! This is it, it's all done.

BO. Please let me help, you said Leonard wouldn't like you like this and we need him, so I can go to school, just some days, please, Mummy.

JILL pulls BO backwards, offstage. CAROL lays BETH down. JILL and CAROL exit.

BETH. Beth! How many times?! Oh, I'm falling! Don't leave me!

Film in. A beach with seabirds circling. Bo is running, fast, straight towards us down the beach.

BO (*calling as she's forced to exit*). I'll never ever leave you!

Scene Eight

BETH's *death rattle.* JILL *enters, to wait beside the bed.* **On film, Bo's arriving at the camera, her body blacks out the shot.** *On stage,* BO *enters, running.* **Film out.** *Then utterly still.*

JILL. You just missed Dominic, he popped for a coffee.

BO. I'm here. Oh, Beth. Oh.

> JILL *leaves.* BETH's *death-rattle breathing, for the longest hardest time.* BO *moves to beside* BETH's *head, she crouches.*

Let go. I'm taking your head. Just let go. Let your body float. You're still here but it'll feel like flying in a dream.

BO's cradling BETH's head.

You can do it.

BETH's *death rattle.*

Breathe out in a long puff.

Death rattle.

Pretend your head's a sack of sand getting wetter and wetter. Heavier head, give your head to me, that's it. There we go.

Death rattle.

Grey goose and gander, waft your wings together and carry the good king's daughter over the one-strand river.

> BETH's *been waiting.* BO *holds her breath, holds everything, channelling this moment she has no control over.* BETH's *breathing stops being sucked in. All goes out. And out. And out. Until she stops.*

Flying.

Scene Nine

Light shifts. BETH's *corpse is covered by a sheet.* BO *sits until the stage is still then steps forward.*

KELLY GREEN (*funeral director*) *enters, carrying brochures.*

KELLY. Hello, you must be, um, Bo, is it?

BO. Yup. For my sins. Hi.

KELLY. Hi, I'm Kelly Green of /

BO. / Green's Funerals, by any chance?

KELLY. I'm sorry your mother died.

BO. Yes. So am I. Amazingly.

KELLY. Yes, well. I have some forms I need filling. All very standard stuff but I do also have these for you to look at – (*Hands over brochures of coffins.*) Have you had any thoughts about the service?

BO. I have thought about nothing else. I want to see her, please? Is she ready? Can I see her now? Don't need those. I want a willow coffin. I'm gonna make me a willow cabin at her gate and call upon my soul within the house. Halloo her name, cos she wouldn't let me call her Mummy, halloo her name to the reverberate hills. And I have these, for the, what do we call it? Programme?

Hands KELLY *photos.*

I don't want a photocopied sheet, I want thick, creamy paper and I want it hand-printed and I want the lettering to be egg yellow, sunshine yellow, cover the same and make sure it's bound together with yarn, here, use this –

Hands skein of wool died with onion skins.

– and, have you got a pen?

KELLY *arms herself.*

I am carrying her in and you can too? Can you do that?

KELLY *nods*.

I want it to be gals at the front, fellas at the rear and I am going to decorate her coffin and I am going to speak. I've written a list, she used to write a lot of lists, I'm going to read it. I want a flash mob to strike up, when I lift her onto my shoulders, singing slow and solemn to start but then totally rocking the kasbah when we hit the actual room, trumpets, accordions, mouth organs, everyone has to be singing, loud. 'When You Smile' – Shirley Bassey arrangement, it's got more bounce. My man's going to pretend to be the vicar. He loved my mum. I want Debussy too. She played the flute when she was a kid. She did so many things, so much. And then not. I want her out of the not. I need to see her. Can I see her now?

KELLY *nods*.

KELLY. Yes, I got her ready myself. She's very beautiful, isn't she?

BO. I knew I'd chosen the right woman for the job, she'd have loved you. And look.

BO *picks up* BETH*'s shawl*.

She made this. I need her wrapped up tight and warm in this, please.

KELLY. That is, just, lovely. You ready?

BO. I very much am.

KELLY *exits*.

Scene Ten

BO *alone*.

Film fades up. Beth's willow coffin, in situ at her funeral. The coffin's draped in Beth's rug, which used to live under the table in Skylar's bedroom.

BO. Thank you all for coming.

BO *takes pages from a notebook, she's about to read, then doesn't*.

During the drives, these last three weeks of Beth's life, between her and back home, I've been thinking about how hard I've tried, over the last thirty years, to forget. I was wrong to do that. Turns out memories, no matter what form they visit you in, are… everything. So, lest I ever forget again.

She reads.

Some Things My Mother Taught Me.
How a sewing machine works, how to thread one and how to sew.
That you need cold hands to make perfect pastry.
How to apply lipstick, red.
How to look at something and see how it works.
That you can always make a version of the thing you desire but can't afford.
How to knit, darn and crochet.
How to build a bonfire.
How to prune a rosebush, plant bulbs for spring, put marigolds in your carrot patch.
What a maraschino cherry is for.
That life is for living.
How to blow smoke rings.
How to live without her.
How to soothe a fevered brow.
How to mix paint so your walls are exactly the colour you need.
How to make a dye from onion skins.
How to drag a mattress onto the lawn to sleep out, when there are shooting stars.

That cold baths electrify the soul.
How not to incur her wrath.
That you can grow an avocado tree (small) from their stones.
How to be perpetually late and still have a room enchanted by your, eventual, entrance.
How to clip a chicken's wings to stop it escaping.
How to get nits out of hair.
How to raise one ironic eyebrow.
The very best way to eat an orange.
How to take care.
How to be fierce.
That you need ice-cold water to get burnt sugar off a pan.
How to make a living from pretend.
How to survive the sleepless nights.
That only boring people get bored, make something.
How to live with fear, just.
To see beauty in crazy places.
That I am on my own.
How to cherish a daughter.
The power of womanhood.
The power of the list.
How to mix cement and build a wall.
How to be a snob and how to care not a jittery jot about colour or class.
How to cook without recipes but always weigh stuff when baking.
How to join in with singing.
That life isn't fair.
That crying is good.
How to remove a splinter.
How to cope with stampeding cows.
That home-made ginger beer can cause havoc, if left un-drunk.
How to make the cry of an owl by curling up your tongue.
That eggs make an excellent conditioner for your hair but don't use hot water to wash, for obvious reasons.
How to use a baking tray as a sledge.
How to look on the bright side.
And now, how to die.

The swimming/dance music plays, as an echo. BO *folds her list, movement catches her eye. From the back of the auditorium,* SKYLAR (*eight*) *runs at her mum, smashes her body into* BO, *buries her face into her.* BO *holds her daughter tight. The music plays.* BO *looks up and forwards.* **Light fades on stage and film.**

The End.

A Note for Future Productions

As the play progresses, the filmed scenes, which show Bo's memories, become abstracted, less literal, as memory, encoded in the body, reveals itself in different ways. The linking element with the onstage action, is a quality of light. In the original production we used a number of approaches to filming. Any future production might use an iPhone for the above-water scenes, and a GoPro or an iPhone in a waterproof casing to film the water scenes.